*A*n Enduring Embrace

*Experiencing the
Love
at the Heart
of Prayer*

by

Juanita Ryan

ISBN-13: 978-1478233169

Printed in the United States of America

To Jonah and Iris

CONTENTS

PREFACE

Something seems to have gone wrong with prayer. Prayer is a gift to us from God designed to bring life and hope, peace and joy. But it has, instead, become for many, something burdensome, even tedious.

It is often said that prayer is about having a relationship with God. But we may unknowingly be having a relationship with gods who frighten us—the bully god, the god-who-is-impossible-to-please, the god-who-abandons, the god-who-is-far-away. Being in any kind of relationship with such gods does not provide life, hope, peace or joy.

As a result, prayer can become reduced to something that is constricted and empty. We may find ourselves praying to get things. Or praying in an attempt to obligate God or to control God's mood. Praying to impress God, or to impress others. Praying to make sure God still likes us. Praying because if we don't pray we feel guilty. Praying because it is what is expected of us.

We find ourselves praying without awe, without joy, without honesty and, sadly, often praying without hope and without a sense of the Love who is at the heart of all prayer.

The priceless gift that prayer was meant to be needs to be recovered.

What if we began this journey of recovering the gift of prayer with what Scripture shows us, and what Jesus lived for us, about who God is? What if it is true that God is love, that God's love is unfailing towards all God has made? What if God truly is full of compassion and mercy? What if God is the Giver of every good and perfect gift? What if the One who made us longs for relationship with us?

What if we then began to understand prayer to be a loving conversation, a glorious song, a joyful dance, a safe and enduring

1

embrace, initiated and sustained by our Maker? What if prayer were as natural to us as breathing in and breathing out the life and love of God?

What if all of what we are and all that we experience is welcomed by the God who made us and loves us? What if our Maker longs for us to bring all our doubts and fears and resistance, all our questions, all our failings, all our longings and confusion, all our need, all of ourselves to this relationship?

What if prayer is not something we do to try to reach a god-who-is-far-away, but is, instead the endless movements of grace coming from the heart of the God-who-is-near? What if prayer is God calling to us, God singing over us, God giving voice to our groanings that are too painful for us to put into words, God offering to forgive us and change us and free us, God inviting us into the heart of Love?

What if our part in prayer is our response to this flow of grace? What if it is our struggle, our acknowledgment, our surrender to love, our consenting to allow love to transform us?

What if prayer is not only our conversations with God, but our life with God? What if it is the response not only of our lips and hearts, but of our whole lives? What if? Imagine.

An Enduring Embrace is a book of meditations and suggestions for prayer. It is designed to throw open new windows and doors in our minds and hearts so that we can experience prayer in the fresh light of God's love in action. It is designed to help us breathe in more fully the life-giving love of God and breathe out that love to others.

My prayer is that working through this book will help you experience prayer in new ways. More as a way of life than as an event. More as a child responding to being embraced by arms of love, than as a religious activity. More as the stillness at the heart of a dance than the performance of the dance. I hope that what you will find here will help you pray more honestly, freely and joyfully. With less of a sense of obligation.

An Enduring Embrace is arranged in sections that reflect, in part, the dance of grace. You can read the meditations in the order they are printed. Or you may want to read them as you are drawn to the titles—emphasizing ones that speak to your experience or need at the current moment.

However you choose to use this book, do your best to go gently. Read a single meditation. Sit with it. Hold it. Let it hold you. Open your hands and heart to receive what you are being shown. Breathe in God's word to you throughout the day and during the waking moments of the night. Invite the Spirit to open your spiritual lungs to breathe more deeply this particular grace and truth. Let yourself live it. Let it live in you. There is no hurry.

For those who are helped by writing, you might want to write about your own experiences with the Love at the heart of prayer. Notes kept along the way can help the gifts of fresh breath fill your body and mind and heart.

Do, please, keep in mind that these meditations and suggestions are not hoops to jump through or things to check off of a to-do list. They are ways of inhaling and exhaling more fully the life and love and goodness of God.

However you approach this book, know that God has been loving you, drawing you, singing over you, breathing into you all of your life. Know that there is more—always, always more—of grace and goodness to breathe in and to breathe out. Quiet yourself for a moment and breathe in, inviting that more that God has for you today. And breathe out. You are loved beyond telling.

Juanita Ryan

3

INTRODUCTION

*The Lord God formed the man from the dust of the ground
and breathed into his nostrils the breath of life
and the man became a living being.*
Genesis 2:7

God breathes out. We breathe in. And we live. Our life, a gift. Each breath, a new gift. We live and move and have our being through the life support of our Maker. All of life is lived in relationship to this One who breathes out life so that we can breathe in life.

Life lived in relationship to our Maker is prayer. All of life, all our life, is a gift received, a prayer lived. This is perhaps the broadest and deepest meaning of what it is to live and what it is to pray. It all begins with God. All life. All prayer.

God is the initiator. We, the creatures, are the responders. God breathes out. We breathe in and live. God, who is with us always, calls us, longs for us, seeks fuller relationship with us. By God's grace, we acknowledge the Giver of all good gifts and receive more fully. We begin to enter a more fully conscious, open hearted relationship with this One on whom our every breath depends. And we are changed. We are freed to be our creature-selves—dependant, child-like, teachable, honest, humble. And into this opening vessel, grace rushes, filling us with the light and life and goodness of God so that God can be more fully present in us and in the world through us. This is prayer.

Prayer is a living, dynamic reality. It is all the rhythms of life lived in relationship with the One who gives us life. It is our service and our rest. Our work and our celebration. Our solitude and our community with others. Our extending grace and our need for grace. Our silence and the out pouring of our hearts.

5

Our lament and our great joy. Our letting go and our holding fast. It is all prayer.

There is a problem, however. There are forces at play in our world and in our lives that cause us to lose sight of who our Maker is, of who we are and of who our neighbor is. We lose sight of the most basic realities: that we all are loved and valued beyond telling by our Maker, that all of life was designed to be lived in loving relationship with God and with each other. Because we lose our way, we fail to love. We miss the mark. We hurt ourselves and each other. The beauty of God's life in us is dimmed, even eclipsed. We find ourselves in the dark, afraid and defended, full of resentment and despair.

We need to be awakened from our sleep of forgetfulness. We need new eyes to see, new ears to hear, new hearts and minds to respond to the call of love from God. We need to be healed, forgiven, helped and guided. We need to be set free.

This, too, is God's amazing initiative. The Christian story is the story of God sending Jesus, of God coming to us in Jesus. Jesus came, not to judge, but to save, to heal, to set free. Jesus came to declare to us that God, our Maker, loves and values us beyond our comprehension. Jesus came to show us the way of true life, surrendered to God, the way of true self-giving love. Jesus came to wake us up, to give us new eyes and hearts, to save us from our worst selves, and to free us to be our true selves— made in God's own image.

God sustains us with the breath of life and calls us through Scripture, through the good news of Jesus, through the wind of the Spirit moving in our world and our lives. God calls us through our longings, our need, our failings and through gifts and grace flowing from God's heart of love.

Even as God breathes each breath into us, God also seeks to wake us up to the fullness of life. "Breathe Me in more deeply,"

God says to us. "Let your heart wake up to its longing for Me, its longing for love. In humility and honesty, acknowledge your failures to love and your need of Me. Turn to Me, I am right here. Let all of life be lived in an unfolding relationship of love with Me and with others."

The dynamic of life and of prayer is that God breathes and we live. God calls us in love to come closer and we find our hearts longing for God. God pours out God's Self and our lives are touched in ways unlooked for, unexpected. We struggle and fall and call out for help, only to realize that Someone has been waiting for our call all along. The wind of the Spirit blows and we wake to the windows of our soul blown open and the light of God pouring in. In this light we know ourselves in all our complexity—beautiful in our making, marred and hurtful in our selfishness and greed and pride, loved and valued beyond our comprehension. Jesus comes and kneels before us, a Joyful Servant, and we see how much we hold back love from others, and how much our spirits long to kneel with Jesus before all others in joyful service.

We are partners in a dance. A dance in which we are clearly not in the lead. We are the responders, the receivers, and also often the resisters, of these endless movements of grace. As we dance in these ways with God, and learn to resist less and less, we begin to hear the love song our Maker continually sings over us and our hearts respond with songs of love in return. Our hearts open. And gratitude pours out, and joy. We experience the truth of who we are, that we are the much loved children of God. We are ready now to turn more often and more freely to God for comfort when we sorrow, for strength when we suffer, for forgiveness when we fail, for guidance in all our affairs. We are changing. We are being set free to know that we are loved. We are being freed to love. Breathing in the life and love that is God, breathing out the love of God to others.

Prayer As God's Initiative

The unfolding narrative of Scripture is a narrative of God in action. God moves, creates, breathes life. God loves, provides, seeks, instructs, delivers, leads. God pursues, opposes evil, forgives, heals. God sends, comes, lives with us, reconciles. God acts.

The subplot to this story is our part. We breathe in God's life and live. We struggle, resist, acknowledge, respond, fail, fall, confess, bow, open our hearts, receive, awaken, change.

Our praying is always the second movement in the experience of prayer. It is always a response to the God who is already acting on our behalf. When we pray we are not the initiators, reaching out to a God who is far away, or to a God who is unmoved and unmoving. When we pray it is because the Mover and Maker of all is moving in us and around us and our spirits are responding.

When we see prayer from this vantage point it changes everything. The perspective of prayer as our effort to reach God or to convince God of our need or to be seen or heard by God, is undone. Instead, prayer is God reaching out to us, seeing us always, hearing us always, and always moving in faithful loving kindness to heal and bless us.

Our part in prayer becomes almost effortless. We hear knocking at the door and say, "Come in." We are full of shame, walking alone, and see One running full speed toward us, and suddenly, unexpectedly, we are being honored, embraced, celebrated. We have no words, no way to pray and find that the Spirit is praying with compassionate groans on our behalf. We feel forgotten, unseen, unheard only to discover that God always pursues us, always sees us, always hears us and loves us beyond our wildest imaginations.

Even as our breath is a response to God's breath in us, our prayer is a response to God's call of love and joy over us. May you breathe deeply of this Life, this Love, poured out to you.

God Initiating Respectfully As Prayer

Here I am! I stand at the door and knock.
If anyone hears my voice and opens the door,
I will come in and eat with him and he with me.
Revelations 3:20

We think of prayer as something we initiate. We call out to God and we hope that God will hear us. But we are not the initiators of prayer. God is. It is God who comes to us. It is God who knocks on the door of our hearts and says, "I desire a relationship with you, can I come in?"

Whether we know it or not, our prayers are a response to God's knocking. We may not even hear the knock, but something in us stirs us to pray. A need, a longing, a faint hope, a desperation may move us to go to the door and open it to God.

Sometimes this text is read as if it referred to a one time event. God knocks, we let God in and now all is well. But it can also be seen as more of an ongoing reality. We get distracted by the cares of life, by our own agenda, by a hundred different things and forget our need and longing for a relationship with God. But all the time, God is there, reminding us, knocking at the door, waiting to come in.

The image of God in this text is surprising, even shocking. The first surprise is that God is not far away. God is not unreachable. God says to us, "Here I am!" God is right here with us.

A second surprise is that God shows us respect. God knocks. God does not barge in. God does not demand. God does not disrespect our boundaries. God knocks.

A third surprise is that God waits. We often lament how difficult it is for us to wait for God to respond to us. But the truth is, that more often than not, it is God who is doing the waiting. It is God who waits for us to answer.

A fourth surprise is this image of a God who desires to come into the middle of our lives, no matter what kind of a mess we might be in. We do not have to clean house before we open the door. God invites us to open the door, no matter what is happening in our lives.

Finally, we see here a God who asks to sit at the kitchen table with us in order to share a meal with us. This is an image of relaxed friendship, of ease. God seeks relationship with us. God seeks intimacy with us.

How is it that the Maker of all that exists, the One who sustains our life from breath to breath is the one who humbly, respectfully knocks at the door of our heart and waits, all the while expressing a vulnerable longing for intimacy with us? This is an image of a God who is humble, a God who comes disguised as a beggar at our door, looking for a meal, looking for a home.

It is also an image of a God who is all that love is. Patient. Kind. Respectful. Never losing hope. This is the One who knocks and waits. This is the One who desires relationship with us. To this One we can respond, knowing we are safe, knowing we are loved.

God stands at the door and knocks and waits.

Prayer begins with God's respectful initiation.

You are here,
right here with me,
seeking me,
calling me,
waiting for me to respond
and to invite you into my life today.
You are kind, respectful of me
as you knock and wait.
You say you want to come into the middle of my life,
just like it is.
You ask to sit at the kitchen table with me
and just be with me.
You would like to share a meal with me
and enjoy friendship with me.
To all of this I say yes.
I hear you knocking.
Come in, Lord, come in.

Prayer suggestion:

Sit quietly with this image of God knocking at the door of your life. Notice your responses to this image. When you are ready, respond to God's patient, respectful, loving initiative.

God Running to Embrace Us as Prayer

*So he got up and went to his father. But while he was still
a long way off, his father saw him and was filled with compassion for him; he ran to his son, threw his arms around
him and kissed him.*
Luke 15:20

The young man in this story is returning home. He is desperate. He is homeless. He is starving. He has blown all his
inheritance and made a mess of his life. He is practicing a prayer
of sorts. It goes something like this: "I know I am no good. I
know you don't want to see me or have anything to do with me.
But I am homeless and starving. I was hoping to beg you to let
me be a servant, just to have a bed and some food, that's all."

When we get up and go to God, our true Father, we often do
so with the same mind set as the young man in this story that
Jesus told. Many of us, in the dark corners of our hearts and
minds, carry this kind of fear with us as we approach God. We
are anxious, insecure and troubled when we go to God. We
expect disapproval, disappointment, rejection from God.

What is so difficult for us to comprehend is the God that
Jesus described in this and many other stories. It is difficult to
fully grasp the reality of this God.

What we do not know is that long before we started to try to
formulate some kind of prayer, God had been loving us, longing for us, calling us home, waiting for us, eager to welcome us,
seeing us as a priceless treasure, knowing us each as God's own
beloved child.

All prayer begins with this One. All prayer begins with the
God who waits for us, the God whose arms ache to hold us,
the God whose heart is tender with love for us. This is the God
who runs to us and embraces us while we are still practicing our

speech of a prayer, trying to get it right even as we, in our great shame and fear, get it all wrong.

Jesus' story about the God-who-runs-to-us-and-embraces-us was addressed to a mixed audience. There were both "tax collectors and sinners" and "pharisees and teacher of the law". Both groups no doubt included people who sincerely believed that it was their religious obligation to "get things right" so that God's favor would be secured. And, both groups probably included people who had despaired of ever being good enough to please God.

In telling this story Jesus was speaking the truth of God's unfailing love directly to the hearts of both groups. They may have grown up with biological or spiritual fathers who filled them with fear about God and with shame about themselves. "But," Jesus said, "let me give you a picture of your true Father. God, your Father, is not what you fear God to be. God is a Father who runs to embrace you. God sees you a long way off, and with a heart full of joy, God runs to you, moving with great speed to wrap arms of love around you."

This image was even more stunning to Jesus' audience at the time than it is to us because well-to-do men of that time did not run. Only servants ran. This God, whom Jesus longs for us to know, is a Servant Father. And this Servant Father is demonstratively emotional and affectionate toward us. This is a Father who is openly, unashamedly crazy in love with us.

Prayer begins with God who sees us with compassion and runs to embrace us.

I come to you with
all kinds of fears
and uncertainties.
I am convinced that you must be disappointed in me.
I fear you will reject me.
But you surprise me.
You shock me.
You almost knock me over
with your exuberance.
You run to me, God.
You throw your arms around me.
You kiss me.
You call me your own.
You tell me that you have been calling me,
longing for me, waiting eagerly for me.
before I ever had a thought about You.
Help me to receive you, God.
You who have run to embrace me.
May I rest in your embrace.

Prayer suggestion:

Sit quietly for a few moments. Take some easy, deep breaths, allowing your heart and mind to become quiet. See yourself on a path. You are lost. You are uncertain. You long to know God as your true Father, but you anticipate disappointment and rejection. You look down the road and see someone running toward you. This One is moving fast. You realize to your shock that this One who runs toward you with joy is God. God's arms are stretched out toward you. God calls your name. You see joy on God's face. You hear God say "my child" to you. God is in front of you now, embracing you, kissing your cheek. Let God hold you. Take some time to tell God anything you want to say. Listen as God speaks love to you.

God Expressing for Us What We Cannot Express as Prayer

In the same way, the Spirit helps us in our weakness.
We do not know what we ought to pray for,
but the Spirit himself intercedes for us
with groans that words cannot express.
Romans 8:26

Sometimes prayer is God expressing for us what we cannot express. It is not uncommon for us to think of prayer as something we have to do on our own power. This way of thinking of prayer often includes the mistaken belief that we have to know what to ask for or what to say before we talk with God.

But there are many times in life when situations are overwhelming or distressing, or we are lost and confused. In those times we don't have any idea what it would mean to pray. No words come. As a result, we may inadvertently shut our hearts and minds and turn our backs to any possibility of prayer. We may deny, or minimize, or intellectualize about the situation and not even think of praying.

The amazing truth is that God invites us to stay prayerful even when we don't know how to pray. Even when we are overwhelmed or lost or confused. Even when we have been rendered speechless. Even when we don't have any sense at all about "what we ought to pray for," God invites us to stay present to the reality of the situation and to God. God invites us to keep our hearts and minds open. God tells us that we can allow the Spirit to pray for us and for the situation, and that the Spirit's prayer becomes our own.

Our tendency as humans is to rely on ourselves. We think we have to figure things out and make things happen. Even prayer is something we rely on ourselves to do.

But God is always calling us to give up our self-reliance and to actively seek counsel, wisdom and guidance from God. This means that even our praying is not all on our shoulders. Even praying is something that God wants to teach us and guide us to do. But more than that, praying is something that God wants to do in us and through us.

In this prayer of not knowing how to pray we are reminded that all of life is meant to be lived in reliance on God. We are also reminded that God's wisdom and knowledge are far beyond our own. And we are reminded that God knows us intimately and personally. We are not alone. God is with us and actively for us, praying for us and through us even when we don't know how to pray.

The prayer of God expressing for us what we don't know how to express is a prayer of trust, of surrender, of humility. It is the prayer of staying open in our weakness to the power and the love of God working and praying through us and for us.

Sometimes I don't know how to pray.
Sometimes I think I know
when really I don't.
Thank you that it is okay to be at a loss.
Thank you that when I am speechless,
when I am uncertain or overwhelmed,
and do not know how to pray or what to pray
that your Spirit prays for me
with great wisdom and knowledge,
with deep understanding and love.
Help me to keep my heart and mind open
to you
in prayerful awareness
even when I don't know how to pray.
Thank you that you, Spirit,
pray for me and through me.

Prayer suggestion:

In a time of quiet ask God to show you where you have closed your heart and mind to the possibility of prayer because you did not know what to pray. Ask for the grace to be open in your weakness to allowing the Spirit to pray for you.

Being pursued by God as prayer

Suppose a woman has ten silver coins and loses one. Does she not light a lamp, sweep the house and search carefully until she finds it? And when she finds it, she calls her friends and neighbors together and says, "Rejoice with me; I have found my lost coin." In the same way, I tell you, there is rejoicing in the presence of the angels of God over one sinner who repents.
Luke 15: 8-10

The gospel of Luke records a trilogy of Jesus' stories about the God who pursues us when we have lost our way. The trilogy includes a story about a lost son, a lost lamb and a lost coin. The purpose of these stories was to provide glimpses into the heart of God—images of what it might mean to be loved and valued by our Maker.

All of the stories are about a God who does not give up on us but who pursues us in love and compassion. Other people may give up on us. We may give up on ourselves. We may judge ourselves or others as lost causes. But God sees us as priceless treasures and never gives up.

In the story of the lost coin God is like a woman who is sweeping the dusty, dark corners of the house to find the valuable coin. God lights a lamp, sweeps and searches until the coin is found.

The story of the lost coin is striking for several reasons. First of all, God is a woman. God is a woman who needs to clean house. The image of God as a woman would have been beyond outrageous to Jesus' audience. Women in the first century were excluded from education, they could not give testimony in a court of law, they were treated as property. Yet, in this story,

Jesus presents God as a woman in search of a missing coin. This is an astonishing image of a God who humbly, vulnerably puts on an apron, picks up a broom and comes into the mess of our lives to pursue us, rescue us and restore us.

A second interesting feature of this story is that it is a coin that is lost. A coin does not have the capacity to choose to be lost or to choose to be found. A lost coin is powerless to help itself. We do not like to see ourselves in the lost coin. We do not like our powerlessness. We do not like to admit that we have fallen into the dark and dusky corner of shame, fear and despair. We do not like the fact that we are lost in our addictions, obsessions and resentments. But, like the coin, we are spiritually lost and powerless to help ourselves.

This would be a completely hopeless condition except for one thing. There is a Power greater than ourselves who can find and restore us. We are powerless, but God is not. God is powerful. And God never loses sight of us. We have never been lost to God. God, the housewife, knows exactly where to sweep. God knows where we have fallen. And in compassion and kindness God pursues us, sweeping away the dirt and dust that has accumulated during our days in the corner underneath the dresser.

Imagine for a the moment the instant when this persistent, pursuing God finds us. We may fear that all God will see is the dust, the grime. But God sees the full reality of who we are. Watch for a moment as God picks us up. See the joy in God's eyes. Watch as God takes the corner of an apron and gently rubs the grime away so that our true self begins to shine through. Imagine that God is so delighted to have found us that a celestial party is organized.

We may be lost to ourselves. Or lost to others. But God pursues us, finds us, holds us joyfully in powerful, tender hands and faithfully restores us.

It is painful to know myself to be the coin
lost in a dark corner,
covered with grime,
unable to get myself out of the darkness.
You put on an apron and pick up a broom.
You sweep. You find the hidden place.
You see me in spite of the dust and dirt.
You pick me up.
You take the corner of your apron
and begin to wipe away the grime.
You joyfully hold me in your mighty, tender hands.
You restore me.
And angels celebrate.

Suggestion for prayer

Sit quietly, breathe slowly and easily for a few minutes. Let your heart and mind sit with the story of the Woman who lights the lamp, puts on an apron, picks up a broom and comes looking for you in the dark corner where you have fallen. Let yourself be held in the powerful hands that have found you. Allow God to gently remove the grime so that you shine through. Admit to God your powerlessness over your spiritual brokenness. Acknowledge that God is powerful and able to restore you. Thank God for pursuing you, holding you, restoring you, celebrating you.

Being Seen by God as Prayer

She gave this name to the Lord who spoke to her,
You are the God who sees me, for she said,
I have now seen the One who sees me.
Genesis 16:13

This prayer, recorded in Genesis 16, is the prayer of Hagar, the Egyptian servant of Abraham and Sarah. Years after God had promised Abraham and Sarah children, and no children had come, they took it upon themselves to "build a family through" this servant girl. And so it was that Hagar bore Abraham a son named Ishmael. The day came, however, when Sarah gave birth to the son she had been promised, and she felt threatened by Ishmael. So she had Abraham send Hagar and Ishmael out into the desert. They were disowned, devalued, abandoned.

Left alone in the desert to die, Hagar cried out to God to save her son. In response to her cry, God showed Hagar two things. God showed her a well of water nearby. And God showed her that she was not alone. Others may have rejected and abandoned her. Others may not have seen her. But God saw her. God saw her and her son through eyes of love and compassion.

Hagar's response to God's loving care is to give God a new name. She calls God, the "God-who-sees-me." Hagar says, "I have seen the One who sees me."

Prayer is being seen by God. And, prayer is seeing the One who sees us. Prayer is knowing that we are seen by God.

To be seen through eyes of love is, perhaps, our most fundamental need. Healthy parents are able to do this for their children. They look at them and see them. They see their child's needs, feelings, limits, strengths, uniqueness. They see their children's preciousness. They see their children with delight, empathy and tender affection.

This is the soil in which healthy children grow. Children who know they are seen and loved. Children who are free to see and love others.

Unfortunately, many of us did not receive this gift of being seen through eyes of love in our biological families. We may not know what it is to feel seen. We may not know what is was for our needs and feelings, our limits and gifts, our uniqueness and value to be seen. We may feel invisible.

Some of us may prefer to remain invisible. Some of us want only to hide. Being seen in the past may have meant being hurt. But if this were the case, we were never truly seen. To be truly seen is to be seen for who we really are as God's much loved children. To be truly seen is to be valued. It is to be loved.

God is the God-who-sees-us. God sees our needs, our deepest fears and longings, our limits, our strengths, our uniqueness, our value. God sees us through eyes of love. God gazes on us in love.

Prayer is being seen by the One-who-sees-us through eyes of love.

You see me.

I am not invisible to you.

I am not overlooked by you.

You see me.

And, just like you saw Hagar,

with love and compassion,

you see me,

through eyes of love.

You see me deeply.

You see my longings, my fears

my desires, my love, my spirit.

You see me

and I know more fully that I am.

I am because you gave me life.

I am because you sustain me with your love.

I am because you see me.

Prayer suggestion:

Sit quietly, breathing slowly, with your hands open on your lap in a receptive posture. Be aware of the Presence of kindness and compassion. Be aware that this is God with you, seeing you through eyes of love. Allow yourself to be seen by the One who sees you with compassion and delight.

Being Heard by God as Prayer

Give ear to my words, O Lord,
consider my sighing.
Listen to my cry for help,
my King and my God,
for to you I pray.
In the morning, O Lord, you hear my voice;
in the morning I lay my requests before you
and wait in expectation.
Psalm 5:1-3

Prayer is being heard by God. Prayer is based on the amazing reality that God hears us. God hears our words. God hears our hearts. As the psalmist says, God hears our sighing, our cries for help, our requests.

Being deeply, accurately heard is vital to any relationship. To know that our hearts are being heard is to have the experience of being known. To know that our hearts are heard and that we are met with empathy and compassion is to know that we are loved.

What the psalmist is affirming in this text is that God always hears us deeply, accurately, with empathy and compassion. Our sighs, our cries for help, our requests all matter to God because we matter to God.

It is not always easy to trust that this is true. It is not easy to trust that our words and our hearts are heard by our Maker. Sometimes we may pray with great passion and urgency. Sometimes we may pray with great hesitation and uncertainty. Either way, we may find ourselves wondering if we are fooling ourselves by imagining that our prayers are being heard.

Most people of faith, most people who have ever prayed, have times of doubt about being heard by God. We may fear that God is not listening, that God does not care, that we are not good enough, or that our prayers are not good enough, to matter to God.

But these fears are rooted in our experiences with other humans. They are not rooted in who God is. God is a God who has promised to hear our prayers with love and compassion.

When the Israelites of long ago struggled to trust that God heard their prayers, they would sometimes review together the ways they had seen God respond to their prayers in the past. Together they would review these times in order to better rest in the promise that God is a God who hears.

This is something that would also be good for us to do. It can be helpful to review the times when we have experienced God's response to the cries of our heart. Times that confirmed to us that we are heard, that we matter.

God is a God who hears. Our prayers are received by the loving, tender heart of God. Prayer is the amazing reality of God hearing us.

You are the-God-who-hears.
You hear my words.
You hear my sighs, my cries for help,
my requests.
You hear me with a loving,
compassionate, caring heart.
Strengthen my faith.
Remind me of all the ways
I have experienced you
responding to me,
all the times I have seen
the evidence that you have heard me.
Thank you for hearing me.
Thank you for hearing me
with a heart of love.

Prayer suggestion:

As you sit in quiet, reflect for a few moments on the-God-who-hears. Reflect on the God-who-hears your sighs and cries for help with compassion. As you are ready, speak your heart to God. Thank God for hearing you today.

Prayer as Struggling with God

God initiates relationship with us. God calls to us in love. But we fear that it is too good to be true. We hesitate to trust that we are known and loved and valued by our Maker. So we struggle. We question the suffering in our lives and in the lives of those we love. We protest the injustice and violence in the world that God does not seem to stop. We doubt the promise of blessing God speaks to us. We come to realize that we live with attachments to gods who are not God—gods who are abusive, abandoning, impossible to please.

God initiates in love and longing. And we resist. We refuse the dance. So many questions and doubts stand in the way. Yet our spirits long to be with this One who is love itself.

What we may not realize is that even in our struggle we are not alone. God invites us to bring our questions and protests and doubts and longings and false attachments into the light of God's grace and goodness. God does not abandon us to struggle on our own. God keeps listening to us, hearing us and responding to us in compassion.

Our struggles with God are a vital part of prayer.

Questioning God as Prayer

Why, O Lord, do you stand far off?
Why do you hide yourself in times of trouble?
Psalm 10:1

The psalmist addressed urgent questions to God. Where are you God? Where are you when we really need you? Why do you hide yourself in times of trouble?

These are desperate, challenging questions. The psalmist is not posing these questions to a religious leader or scholar in hopes of getting some resolution to a merely intellectual problem. The questions are passionate and personal questions about God that the psalmist is bringing directly to God.

Many of us have ideas about prayer that actually keep us from praying. We may have the idea that we have to be polite or formal or meek when we pray. Or that we have to muster up the right thoughts or feelings. It may not occur to us that we can bring our doubts and fears and terrible questions about God to God.

These unspoken rules about prayer are probably a reflection of what we have been taught about prayer. They may even be a reflection of the unhealthy communication patterns in the families in which we grew up. As we can see from this text from the Psalms, and from many others like it throughout Scripture, these rules are not found in Scripture. Quite the opposite. We are shown over and over again by people of great faith and people struggling with faith, that questioning God is a vital kind of prayer.

For those of us who have ever doubted God's unfailing love for us, this kind of prayer can be frightening. We may imagine that God will respond to our anguished questions about our experience of being abandoned by God with anger and further abandonment. This may be so scary for us that we have a difficult time letting ourselves know that these questions about God exist inside us.

But the truth is that we all experience deep losses in life. We all witness terrible traumas in the lives of others. We suffer unjustly and we don't understand how God can allow this. We need to know that we can rely on God to help us, even if, at times, the evidence seems to suggest that we are on our own.

Terrible suffering and injustices happen in this world all the time. If we aren't distracting ourselves or numbing ourselves to these realities we are likely to find ourselves with questions we want to ask God—questions much like the ones the psalmist asked.

There is nothing easy about these questions. But there are times in our lives when they are the most honest prayer we have. God's desire is for us to bring these urgent, painful questions directly to God in prayer. God wants us to know that this form of prayer is welcome, accepted and even honored by God.

Why?

Why did this happen?

Did you forget me?

Did you forget these others?

Do you not care?

God!

Where are you?

Where have you been?

Prayer suggestion:

Write your own urgent questions about God. What has taken place in your life, in the past or in the present, that has left you with questions about God? Write a prayer describing the specific events and issues that you have faced or are facing. Take some time to see if there is a central question about God which emerges from these reflections. Bring this question about God to God. Let your question be a prayer.

Protest as Prayer

How long, O Lord, must I call for help,
but you do not listen?
Or cry out to you, "Violence!" but you do not save?
Why do you tolerate wrong?
Destruction and violence are before me;
there is strife, and conflict abounds.
Therefore the law is paralyzed,
and justice never prevails.
Habakkuk 1:2-3

These words of protest are not the words of a cynic. They are not the words of a scoffer. These are the words of a prophet of the Lord.

"God do you see? Do you see the violence? Do you see the injustice? If you see it, why do you tolerate it? Why do you not act?"

This protest is an expression of a passionate longing for peace and justice. It is a protest against abuse, greed and corruption of every kind. It is a protest against violence and oppression of every kind.

We long for peace. We long for justice. For ourselves, for our families and for our communities. But our personal power to bring an end to violence and to establish justice is very limited. We are up against forces that are far more powerful than we are. We need God to act.

Yet God seems, at times, to do nothing.

So we turn, with the prophet, to God and we protest. Our passionate longing for justice spills out. "God we long for justice to be done, we long for peace to prevail. Help us!" we pray.

We may expect that our prayer of protest will be difficult for

God to hear. But our prayers of protest against injustice and violence are welcomed by God. Scripture teaches us that justice and peace are some of God's deepest passions. It may well be, therefore, that when we pray prayers of protest that it is God's own passions at work within us, moving us, empowering us, drawing us ever more closely together.

When we open our hearts to our own experiences of suffering or to the suffering of others, we begin to feel the same outrage and passionate longing for justice and peace that God experiences. When we take our protest to God, we may find that our protest is flowing from the heart of God.

God, I read and listen to the news,
and I choke on the outrage and helplessness I feel.
The violence in our communities and in our world.
The violence in our homes.
The terrible injustices in this world,
in our own land,
in our own lives.
God, do you see?
God do you know?
Oh, God when will you act?

Prayer suggestion:

Notice the news stories from around the world and in your own community. Ask God's Spirit to draw your attention to one of these stories in particular. Allow yourself to open your heart to the people experiencing violence or injustice. As you are ready, pray a prayer of protest on their behalf. Let yourself long for peace and for justice in this situation.

Or let yourself reflect on whatever violence or injustice that you yourself have suffered. Open your heart to your own suffering. Offer your protest about this suffering to God in prayer, remembering that you and all you feel are safe with God.

Doubt as Prayer

Zechariah asked the angel, "How can I be sure of this?"
Luke 1: 18

We may think of prayer as an act of faith. And so it is. But prayer can also be an honest expression of our uncertainty and doubt.

We want to trust God. We want to have faith. But we have so many questions. So many things are unclear and uncertain. Where do we take our doubts if not to God? Where do we voice our uncertainties if not to God?

Some of us struggle with trusting God's love for us. We believe God is a loving God. But we struggle to trust that God loves us. We may look for ways to erase this doubt. But it is tenacious. We live with the same kind of doubt that Zechariah gave voice to in this text: "How can I be sure of this?'

When Zechariah, a priest, questioned the angel, he was standing in the temple, a holy place. The angel had just told him that he and his elderly wife, who had never been able to have children, were going to have a son who would prepare the way for the Messiah. The angel told him that the prayer that he and his wife had prayed for years, and had long ago given up on, was going to be answered—that the deepest longing of his heart and his wife's heart was going to be met. It was too good to be true. And so, he doubted.

The angel's response to Zechariah's question was to give him a strange kind of gift. Zechariah was given the gift of a sign, a reminder, a promise, that was with him every day until the child was born. The specific sign he was given was that he would not be able to speak until the child was born.. Because the inability to speak is so frightening to us, it might seem like this gift was a kind of punishment for his failure to trust in the good news he had received from the angel.

It is true that the sign of silence might have been particularly challenging for Zechariah because speaking was a central feature of his functions as a priest. Zechariah was a religious professional—one of those people who, just like pastors today, can always be asked to speak, always asked to pray a prayer. People who can always be asked to speak often find it particularly difficult to find room in their lives for not-speaking.

But silence can be a season during which we learn and grow by listening rather than speaking. It can be a kind of reminder that we are more than what we do—that we are more precious than anything we have to say. It is also a reminder that no doubts or fears, no resistance to grace will, in the end, prevent God from giving us the deepest longings of our hearts. No matter how too-good-to-be-true it might seem to us, no matter how speechless it leaves us, God hears our prayers—even when our prayers are full of doubt.

Sometimes prayer is giving voice to our doubts. The things we long to believe may seem too much to hope for, too good to imagine. Even the thought that God might give us what we long for may leave us speechless. But when we voice our doubts, we open a door for God's Spirit to respond with the gifts of grace, truth and healing that we so desperately need.

Prayer is talking with God about our doubts.

I hear your promises
but my heart is closed
in doubt and disbelief.
How can I be certain?
How can I trust that the good things
you say are true?
That you love me?
That you care?
That you are powerful?
How can I know?

Prayer suggestion:

What are your deepest doubts? Voice these doubts to God.
Invite God to respond to your doubts and uncertainties.

Longing as Prayer

As the deer pants for streams of water,
so my soul pants for you, O God.
My soul thirsts for the living God,
When can I go and meet with God?
Psalm 42: 1-2

We can go days, even weeks without food. But we cannot go long without water. Water is a basic survival need. When any of us are deprived of water for a while, our body begins to ache. Our stomach hurts, our head throbs, our mouth and throat are parched deserts. Given enough time, even our kidneys begin to hurt. Our entire body experiences thirst.

The metaphor of thirst in this text is a powerful image of the urgency of our need for God and of our longing for God. Deeper than our questions, deeper than our protest, deeper than our doubts, is our longing for God. Our whole being thirsts for God. Our entire being longs to experience the presence of God.

We long for the One who is our Source, the One who is our heart's true Home, the One who is Love. This is the deepest truth about us. But for too many of us, it is a truth that we cover up and push away.

We come into the world with an urgent thirst for love. It is as real and tangible as our physical thirst. But if our thirst for genuine love is not met by those who care for us, or if this thirst is shamed, or is only responded to when we somehow perform, we shrink from the terrible pain this creates. We harden our longing hearts and tell ourselves that we didn't want love after all. We protect ourselves from the pain of unmet longing by telling ourselves that we don't really need the love of others and we don't really need the tender love of God. We despair that love

41

exists or that it is truly available to us. This despair, as dark as it is, feels more tolerable than our longings.

But burying our longing does not make it go away. It is a core reality that lives and breathes in us. It is central to the way God made us.

Our longing for love may be painful, but when we allow ourselves to experience these longings they offer us the wisdom to seek what we need the most. Like the thirsty deer yearning for water is led to find water, so our thirst for the One who is love, leads us on a quest to find God, as if our lives depended on it.

I ache for you,

I long for you,

I thirst for you.

Where can I find you?

How can I truly know you?

Prayer suggestion:

Sit quietly, asking God's Spirit to reveal your longing for God.

Let the feelings that accompany your longing come to the surface.

As you are able, talk to God about your longing to know God's presence.

Saying No to False Gods as Prayer

Yet my people have forgotten me;
they burn incense to worthless idols,
which made them stumble in their ways.
Jeremiah 18:15

We usually think of prayer as an act of saying "yes" to God. We think of it as saying "yes" to the existence of God and "yes" to a relationship with God.

But too often the God that we are unknowingly saying "yes" to is a god who is made in the image of people who have hurt us or disappointed us. Without realizing it, we often worship and serve false gods. We may intellectually affirm our belief in a God of love, but emotionally we may serve a "worthless idol" who is demanding or abusive or distant. A god who causes us to "stumble on our way."

It is not uncommon for people to unknowingly serve false gods. The god who is punitive, the god who is impossible to please, the god who is unreliable, the god who is passive—all these gods can seem like the true and living God. These "worthless idols" may reflect what we were taught about God. Or they may reflect our private fears about God. Whatever their source, these not-Gods have power over us. But they are not God. They are not the God of unfailing love and grace.

Before we can say "yes" to the God who made us and loves us, we need to begin saying "no" to the false gods we have crafted from our fears and pain. We need to begin to remember the God of love whom we have forgotten. And we need to begin to turn away from the worthless idols who hold us captive and cause us to stumble. This vital work needs to become our prayer.

In saying "no" to false gods, the first step is to acknowledge that these false gods exist and that we have had an impact on our lives. We need to become aware of the discrepancy between the God of love and the idols whom we have worshiped and served.

Acknowledging the presence of these gods in our lives can be painful. We do not want to see this about ourselves. We do not want to see how confused we have become. We do not want to believe that we have forgotten the One true God and have spent our days chasing after idols. But the truth always free us, no matter how painful that truth may be.

When we begin to acknowledge the presence of idolatrous attachments in our lives we can begin the process of saying "no". This, too, may be difficult, because we are afraid of these gods. We are afraid that they are powerful. We are afraid they will punish us or abandon us. We are afraid that if we get rid of them we will have no god at all. And we are afraid to hope that the true God really is loving, really is compassionate, really is on our side.

Sometimes the prayer of saying "no" to the idols we have worshipped is something we have to do many times, even as we ask for gifts of courage and of hope.

God calls us to leave the gods that cause us to stumble and to remember the God of unfailing love.

Prayer is saying "no" to gods who are not God.

I see that I serve worthless idols
that I have crafted from my fears.
Idols who cause me to stumble.
Idols that cause me to forget you.
It is hard to trust that the idols
who are harsh and rejecting
are false
and that you,
Love, are true.
Give me the courage to say no
to my idol gods,
give me hope that your love is real.

Prayer suggestion:

Sit quietly, breathing deeply and easily. Invite God to show you
the idol gods you may be serving. Take some time to observe
these idols. What are they like? How do they compare to the
God of love and grace? How do they cause you to stumble?
Ask the true God of Love to give you the courage and hope you
need to begin to say "no" to these worthless idols. Let your "no"
to these idols be your prayer.

Saying Maybe to the God of Love as Prayer

I do believe;
help me overcome my unbelief.
Mark 9:24

Sometimes prayer is saying "maybe" to God. It is saying "I want to believe you are a God of love, I want to believe you love me, I want to believe you are for me and not against me. Help me to believe these good things about you. Heal the fears I have about you."

We may be guarded and hesitant. Our false and frightening idol gods may haunt us. But when our prayer is the prayer of maybe, we are turning from these idols to the God of love and grace, asking for help to believe in God's goodness and mercy. We may believe intellectually that God is love, but find that we cannot trust that God actually loves us personally. We may want to trust God's personal love for us but realize that we simply cannot.

When we say "maybe" to trusting God's love we acknowledge both our belief and our unbelief. It takes courage to pray this honestly when our heart continues to fear that God might be harsh or abandoning or displeased with us.

But each time we say "maybe" to the God of love, and we experience moments of hope or peace or grace, our courage will grow and our faith will be strengthened.

What we can do is to begin to ask God to help us in our unbelief. We can begin to ask God to open our eyes and ears and heart to know the reality of God's love for us. And then we can listen and watch for God's responses.

These responses from God may come to us in something we read in a book or in a Scripture passage, or in the loving words from a friend. Sometimes the responses we receive from God might be images that came to us in prayer or in the still small voice of the Spirit.

God is eager to "help our unbelief." God will not respond with shame or impatience when we struggle to trust. Instead, God will always respond to our "maybes" with grace and help. And out of these encounters with God's patience and kindness toward us our trust will slowly grow stronger and deeper.

I believe
and yet I don't believe.
I need your help
with my unbelief.
All I am able to do today is to say "maybe".
Maybe I can trust your love.
Open my eyes, open my heart
to know your love.
Accept my prayer of maybe.
It is all I have to offer right now.

Prayer suggestion:

Sit quietly and ask God to show you whatever doubt and fear you experience about God's love. Ask God to help you overcome your unbelief. Offer your prayer of maybe to God.

Prayer as Acknowledging God

All life, all relationship with God, all prayer, begins with our Maker. God creates, breathes life, initiates in love. We resist. We struggle. Yet, even as we struggle, the Spirit pursues in love. And so, in the midst of our questions and doubts we catch glimpses of grace, we see God in action.

We behold the miracle of a new born child. Or gaze at the beauty of the first crocus pushing through the snow, or the first explosion of new green across the landscape in spring. We quiet and sense a small whisper of wonder tugging at us. And we find some part of ourselves responding. We find ourselves acknowledging God.

There are many moments and even many seasons in life of struggling with God. And there are also many moments and seasons during which we acknowledge our Maker. We do not need to judge these complex steps in our dance with God. What we can trust is that in all of the times of struggle and in all of the times of acknowledging, God is with us. God who is Love is with us in all patience, kindness, respect and faithfulness.

When, by grace, we are able to acknowledge our Maker, we are impacted deeply. Our spirits are lifted. And bowed down. We are released. And we are captivated. We see our smallness and our grandeur as God's own children.

Knowing that God is God as Prayer

Know that the LORD is God.
It is he who made us,
and we are his;
we are his people,
the sheep of his pasture.
Psalm 100: 3

Prayer reminds us that God is our Maker. That we belong to God. That God is our Shepherd and we are the sheep of God's pasture. These are truths that prayer helps us to know as living truths.

An important aspect of knowing that God is God, is knowing that we are not God. That may sound pretty obvious but we tend to forget that we are creatures. Knowing that God is God means that we live in the reality that there are things that we do not have the power to do for ourselves or for others. It means that we acknowledge that we are limited. It means remembering that our lives were meant to be lived in loving, joyful dependence on God.

Knowing that God is God also means that our Maker is eager to be our Shepherd. God is eager to guide us, protect us and provide for us, just as a Shepherd cares for his sheep.

In order to let this knowledge become a reality in our lives, we need to begin by letting go of all the ways that we knowingly and unknowingly play God in our own lives and in the lives of others. One way we might do this is by practicing the first three steps of the Twelve Steps of Alcoholics Anonymous—the spiritual practices in these steps can help us whether we are struggling with an addiction or not.

In the first step we admit that we are powerless to control all that is beyond our control. And we admit that trying to control these things leaves our lives unmanageable. For some of us the main issue might be alcohol. For others it might be other people and their behavior. For others it might be a sense of spiritual brokenness. Any time we try to control what we cannot control, we will find ourselves anxious, angry and resentful. And we will find that our lives have gotten out of control. Admitting that we are powerless allows us to return to the basic truth that we are not God.

The second step is coming to believe that there is a Power greater than ourselves who can restore us to sanity. This is the step of acknowledging that there is a God. There is a God who is powerful and who is on our side. A God who longs to restore us to sanity. A God who longs to heal us and help us.

The third step is making the decision (sometimes daily, sometimes hourly) to turn our lives and wills over to God's loving care. This is the step of letting God be God. It may mean turning our addiction or obsession over to God. It may mean turning our loved one over to God's care. It always means turning ourselves over to God's care. It means becoming who we are, the sheep of God's pasture.

Prayer is living in the freeing, healing truth that God is God. And we are not.

All too often
I try to be in charge of things
over which I have no control.
I try to be God in my life
and in other peoples' lives.
I tell myself my intentions are good,
but the truth is that I try to control because I am afraid.
But when I act out of fear I create a bigger mess.
I admit today that only you are God.
I acknowledge that you have power far beyond my own.
I choose to let go of all that is beyond my control..
I entrust my life, my will
and all I care about
to your loving care.

Prayer suggestion:

Ask God to show you all that you are trying to control that is beyond your control. Make a list of what comes to mind. Admit your powerlessness over these things. Acknowledge God's power to restore you and to do what you cannot do. Ask God to give you the grace to entrust your life and will and all that is on your list to God's loving care.

Being Open to Mystery as Prayer

Love never fails.
But where there are prophecies, they will cease;
where there are tongues, they will be stilled;
where there is knowledge, it will pass away.
For we know in part...
Now we see but a poor reflection as in a mirror;
then we shall see face to face.
Now I know in part;
then I shall know fully, even as I am fully known.
And now these three remain; faith, hope and love.
But the greatest of these is love.
I Corinthians 13:8-9a,12-13

When we open ourselves to God in prayer, we encounter mystery. In wonder and awe we open ourselves to our Creator, whom we only know in part.

Mystery is not a part of the spiritual diet many of us were raised on. Many of us have been taught that when it comes to God, it is vital for us to know all the right answers to all the right questions. This leaves little room for mystery. In fact, people who talk about mystery may seem suspect in some way. As a result, God is too often reduced to something that can be controlled, analyzed, intellectualized and contained.

But Scripture teaches us that we see but a poor reflection. We can only know God in part. God is beyond our wildest dreams. God's love and grace and power and beauty and goodness are beyond anything we can imagine.

When we enter a relationship with God in prayer, we enter a relationship with One who cannot be boxed or quantified. We enter a relationship with mystery.

This does not mean that God is unknowable. It does mean

that our knowing will always be limited, especially our intellectual knowledge. So how do we embrace One whom we can only know in part? The answer in this text is that we know with our hearts. We embrace God and God embraces us in love.

The author of the *Cloud of Unknowing,* an anonymous book on contemplative prayer from the 14th century, put it this way:

> He whom neither men nor angels can grasp by knowledge can be embraced by love. For the intellect of both men and angels is too small to comprehend God as he is in himself.... No one can fully comprehend the uncreated God with his knowledge; but each one, in a different way, can grasp him fully through love. (*The Cloud of Unknowing* edited by William Johnston, Image Books, New York, 1973. Page 50,)

When we realize that the "knowing" that Scripture calls us to is the knowing of love, we are freed from the fear and the limitations of having to "understand God correctly." We are freed of our pride and judgments. We are freed to allow the Spirit to continue to teach us. And most of all, we are freed to know ourselves as loved and to love with greater humility and adoration, the One who is our Maker.

Prayer is embracing and being embraced by the mystery that is God.

You are beyond knowledge.
Your love and power and goodness
are too vast for me.
You are beyond my understanding.
Free me from my belief that I need to
analyze and dissect and quantify you.
Free me to humble myself
before the mystery of your Love.
Free me to open my heart
to embrace you
and to be embraced by you,
and thus to encounter you in awe and joy.

Prayer suggestion:

Reflect on all the ways you have experienced yourself embraced by God's love and embracing God in love. Allow yourself to open your heart in love and humility to the God who is mystery.

Bowing as Prayer

But I, by your great mercy,
will come into your house;
in reverence will I bow down
toward your holy temple.
Psalm 5:7

Sometimes when we open ourselves to God in prayer, we remember that we are in the presence of One who is mystery. We acknowledge with awe and wonder that all that God is—all of God's love and goodness and beauty and power—is far beyond our capacity to know or comprehend. As we remember and acknowledge these realities, we bow.

Our bowing in prayer is a physical, as well as a spiritual, act. We may bow our head. We may kneel. We may lie prostrate. However we bow, our bodies express our prayer of reverent awe.

When we bow in prayer, our thoughts are not focused on ourselves or on others. Rather, our hearts and minds are filled with awareness of our Maker. And this awareness changes us.

Sometimes when we sit beside the ocean, or under the stars, or looking out across an open expanse of land, the experience of gazing at something that is vast, beautiful and ancient has a way of bringing things in our lives back into perspective. Problems that seem big begin to seem smaller. Our own disproportionate sense of ourselves comes back into balance. Our view of the world and of life shifts. Humility, peace, surrender, hope and even joy often emerge as a result.

The experience we have when sitting gazing at the beauty of creation is a small glimpse of what can take place as we bow in reverence before our Maker. It is indeed, as the psalmist says, by God's great mercy that we are able to embrace and be embraced by such an experience. When we bow before God, we are drawn out of ourselves, we are moved beyond our thoughts and concerns, we are enlarged.

As we bow in reverence before our Maker, our minds and hearts are captured for a time by this single focus. Albert Edward Day wrote about one such experience he had of bowing in reverence before God:

> In the epiphany of that night of darkness and pain and near despair, the holiness of God became an ecstasy, a captivity of adoration, a heart-smiting and heart-possessing reality. I was caught up and then bowed in enthralled worship.... What I had become aware of thrillingly and exclusively, was a holiness that is wholeness...it was goodness of infinite dimensions, truth transcending all limitations; beauty endlessly satisfying; mercy without limit; forgiveness equal to every desperate sin; restoration transcending every prodigality; wisdom surpassing all human knowledge; everything of value in time and eternity; and always there, without variation, for everybody, in every situation. (Albert Edward Day , *The Captivating Presence,* quoted in *A Guide to Prayer for Ministers and Other Servants*, Reuben P. Job and Norman Shawchuck, The Upper Room, Nashville, Tennessee, 1983, page 244,)

I bow before you.
I bow in reverence
and awe.
I am without words.
Your goodness and love
your beauty and mercy
your power and kindness
leave me breathless.
I bow in silence
before you.

Prayer suggestion:

Read Psalm 8 slowly, prayerfully. Bow in silent reverence
before God. Invite God's Spirit to reveal more of God to you as
you continue to bow for as long as you choose.

Experiencing Awe as Prayer

The heavens declare the glory of God;
the skies proclaim the work of his hands.
Day after day they pour forth speech;
night after night they display knowledge.
There is no speech or language
where their voice is not heard.
Their voice goes out into all the earth,
their words to the ends of the world.
Psalm 19:1-4

Those of us who have lived for years in places where the primary lights in the night sky come from the line up of airplanes approaching the nearest airport may not comprehend the breadth and depth of what the psalmist was expressing in this psalm. But if we have had the opportunity to view the night sky without the intrusion of city lights, even once, we may understand the experience in which such poetry is rooted.

The heavens declare the glory of God. The heavens speak to us in the same language they speak to everyone everywhere. They speak of the grandeur, the power, the beauty of God.

This breathless wonder we experience in response to God's creation is the prayer of awe.

Awe is a prayer we pray not only when we are able to see the vastness of the night sky. It might also be something we experience at surprising times. Awe can take hold of us while gazing at a newborn infant. It can touch us as we witness the transformation of someone once characterized by arrogance into someone who demonstrates open hearted compassion. It can even come in moments of facing a life threatening diagnosis, when the wonder of the gift of life becomes so tangible that we are filled with joy.

Awe moves us out of our myopic perspective—out of our small drama in which we are always at center stage. It moves us to a deeper, fuller vision of who we are as creatures and a deeper, fuller vision of God our Creator.

Awe allows us to glimpse God's beauty, God's power, God's goodness and love.

Awe frees us to let go of trying to play God in our lives and in the lives of others. It frees us to be the dependent creatures we are. It frees us to find joy in the beauty of God.

Much of the time we are like the person who walks along the road of life with our eyes on the path before us, our minds full of our plans and our worries. But once in a while we stop and look around us and above us and we remember. We remember the wonder of the gift of life. We glimpse something of the beauty of God. And we are lifted out of our limited vision at least for a moment. We are lifted into awe.

Maker of all that is,
Creator of the galaxies
Giver of life,
open my eyes
to glimpse your beauty,
your grandeur,
your glory all around me.
Open my mind and heart
in awe.

Prayer suggestion:

Think of a time when you felt awe. Reflect on that time for a few minutes. Allow your mind and heart to respond to the beauty and glory of God.

Worshipping as Prayer

Shout for joy to the Lord, all the earth.
Worship the Lord with gladness;
come before him with joyful songs.
For the Lord is good and his love endures forever,
his faithfulness continues through all generations.
Psalm 100:1, 5

Prayer is worship. But what is worship? And why does God need our worship? I think novelist Marilynne Robinson summarized well what is at the heart of worship.

> "God does not need our worship. We worship to enlarge our sense of the holy, so that we can feel and know the presence of the Lord, who is with us always...Love is what it amounts to, a loftier love, and pleasure in the loving presence." (Marilynne Robinson, *Home*, Farrar, Straus and Giroux, New York, 2008, p 110.)

According to the text from Psalm 100, worship is a response of joyful love to the One who made us. We respond in joyful love because God is good and loving. Our genuine, fully embodied response of love to the One who is love is our worship.

But for many of us worship is something far less than this. For some it is the fearful act of placating a god who demands to be adored. For others it is an act of groveling as unworthy beings before a god who won't even look at us. For others it is a disembodied ritual, an attempt to gain approval from a disapproving god.

But true worship is not placating or groveling or going through the motions. True worship is the activity of people who know they are creatures who belong to their loving Creator.

Worship then becomes a simple, child-like act of responsive joy and gratitude by created beings to their Maker.

This same psalm pictures our relationship with God as being like the relationship between a flock of sheep and a loving Shepherd. The image might be of a group of lambs who have been let out of the barn for the first time. It is spring and they are romping in the meadow under the sun. Their Shepherd is with them and knows them each by name. They do not try to be the shepherd. They are free to be the lambs they are. They know they are safe in the Shepherd's care. They know they belong to their Shepherd. They are free to be fully who they are. Their joy, their gladness is their gift of love to their Shepherd. It is their adoration, their worship.

A similar image might be that of young children, running to the door to throw themselves into their mommy's or daddy's arms the minute they walk into the house. This loving, adoring response is their spontaneous gift of love to their parent. Their parent does not expect this or demand this. But they do receive it with joy. The parent's delight and the child's delight are mingled in these moments in which love is celebrated.

We are God's lambs, we are God's children. We are loved beyond telling. We run to God in joy and gladness. We romp and play near our Shepherd, free and safe and full of adoration for this One who made us and who watches over us. Our glad adoration and love is our worship.

You are God.

All powerful,

all knowing,

all loving.

You made us.

You love us.

You watch over us.

We come to you

with gladness

and joy.

We love you.

We adore you.

Prayer suggestion:

Ask God to guide your heart and mind as you reflect on God as your Maker and as you reflect on God as your Shepherd, who continually cares for you. Allow yourself to respond to God by expressing your love and joy and adoration in whatever way you choose. Your response to God is your prayer of worship.

Praising as Prayer

Praise the LORD, O my soul;
all my inmost being, praise his holy name.
Praise the LORD, O my soul,
and forget not all his benefits-
who forgives all your sins
and heals all your diseases,
who redeems your life from the pit
and crowns you with love and compassion,
who satisfies your desires with good things
so that your youth is renewed like the eagle's.
Psalm 103: 1-5

The prayer of praise is a prayer that focuses not only on God's good gifts to us, but on what those good gifts tell us about God. Praise, then, is the expression of gratitude which focuses on the Giver. It is the joyful celebration of the One who loves us and cares for us.

The act of praise lifts our spirits in loving gratitude to God. Like any experience of gratitude, praise helps us see and take in the good gifts that are being given. But praise takes us one step further, as it opens the eyes of our hearts to see, and acknowledge, the One who is the Source of all good gifts.

The psalmist calls to his soul, to his inmost being, to engage in the act of praise. "Praise the Lord, O my soul," he sings, "Praise his holy name." It is a call to reflect on who God is. It is a call to open one's inmost being in joyful, reverent acknowledgment of God. We do this not because God needs the praise, but because we need to remember who God is.

"Forget not all his benefits," the psalmist continues. The act of remembering who God is, is evidently something we need to consciously, regularly remind ourselves to do. It is too easy to fall into discouragement and despair. It is too easy to become short sighted and forget the big picture. It is too easy to think everything depends on us. It is too easy to doubt that we are truly, intimately loved and cared for by our Maker. It is too easy to forget that God's love is unfailing, powerful, tender, ours. It does our souls good to remember God's kindness and goodness in our lives.

The psalmist then continues by affirming the amazing grace that flows from the heart of God. Who is God? God is the One who forgives all our sins. God is all merciful. God is all compassion. God is a pardoning God. We celebrate God, the Merciful One, and we offer our praise.

Who is God? God is a healing God. It is God who heals all our diseases. All the diseases of our minds. All the diseases of our hearts. All the diseases of our souls. All the diseases of our bodies. We open ourselves in wonder to God our Healer, and we offer our praise.

Who is God? God is the One who restores us. God redeems our lives from the pit and puts a crown of love and compassion on our heads. We allow ourselves to receive this crown from God, our Redeemer, who frees us and loves us, and we offer our praise.

Who is God? God is the One who satisfies our heart's deepest desires with good things. We long to be loved. We long to love. We long to be known and to know. We long for true intimacy with God and with others. God is the One who satisfies these desires, restoring our youth, restoring our hope and our joy. We open our longing hearts to the One who satisfies us, and we offer our praise.

Oh Most merciful God,
you forgive all my self-serving and pride,
all my hurtful, unloving ways,
I praise you for your forgiving heart.
Oh Healer,
you see the diseases of my mind
and heart and body
and you respond with compassion and healing.
I praise you for your healing love.
Oh Redeemer,
you restore me to who you made me to be,
pulling me out of the pit,
placing a crown of love and compassion on my head,
proclaiming that you love me,
that you always have, and always will.
I praise you for your transforming grace.
Oh Provider,
you satisfy my heart's deepest desire
for intimacy with you and with others.
I praise you for your abundant blessings.
I praise you.

Prayer suggestion:

Focus on what this text from Psalm 103 tell us about who God is. Ask God to remove whatever barriers of fear or disbelief there might be in your heart or mind to knowing God in this way. As you are ready, offer your praise to God for who God is.

Prayer as Living in Relationship with God

Prayer has nothing to do with a certain set of words or a specific posture. It is not a magic wand. It is not another way to try to be in charge of things or to earn points with God.

Prayer is breathing in the breath of life and acknowledging the Giver of that life. It is entering the dance with God.

Prayer is the unfolding of a relationship. It is a two way conversation initiated by our Maker. A conversation that leads to ease of communication and to peaceful silences. It is the amazing journey of discovery—of who we are, of who God is, of who our neighbor is. It is the ongoing adventure of living life in relationship to our loving God.

Like any relationship, there are seasons to prayer. Times when we pour out our hearts and times when we listen. Times when we struggle, times when we rest. Times when there seems to be distance and times when we experience intimacy.

But unlike any other relationship, the One with whom we are building a relationship is perfect in love. This One is faithful, constant, steadfast in love that is unconditional, powerful, personal and tender. As a result, this relationship can be relied on like no other. And this relationship will challenge us and change us like no other. Because perfect love works tirelessly to heal all fear and to free us to love like God loves.

Making Conscious Contact with God as Prayer

This is what the Lord says, he who made the earth,
the Lord who formed it and established it—
the Lord is his name.
Call to me and I will answer you
and tell you great and unsearchable things
you do not know.
Jeremiah 33:2-3

Sometimes we turn prayer into something much smaller than it is. Sometimes we treat prayer as if it were the spiritual equivalent of throwing a penny into a wishing well. We say some words and hope our wishes will come true. Or we may turn prayer into a rote exercise. Prayer becomes something we do as a performance because we think it is what is expected of us by God or by others. Or we may treat prayer like a to-do list we create for God. We hand God our list of what we think needs to be done and walk away, hoping our "prayers" will be answered.

But prayer is not the making of a wish, or an empty ritual, or a to-do list for God. Prayer is the conscious act of seeking contact with the true and living God. It is nothing less than this.

Prayer is direct contact with God. And because this is the essence of prayer, prayer is truly a radical, breathtaking and potentially life changing activity. It is an activity that God urges us to do. "Call to me," God says. The One our heart longs for, the One we seek, is eager to hear from us and eager to respond.

There are no qualifiers here, no complications, no hoops to jump through. God gives us a clear invitation: "Call to Me." Call to the One who made the earth, the One who formed it and established it. The God of all, our Maker, is that available to us.

And when we do make contact with God, when we call on

God, God promises to respond. "Call to me, and I will answer you," God says.

To pray is to come as a creature to our Creator. It is to come with a teachable spirit before the One who "formed and established the earth." We do not seek contact with God to instruct God or to placate God, but to have conscious contact with the Love that is at the heart of prayer.

We call to God. And the true and living God answers us. God answers us, not by approving our rituals or scrambling to do the items on our to-do lists. God answers us by revealing to us "great and unsearchable things".

This is the essence of prayer. God calls to us, inviting us to be in relationship. We respond and call on God. And God answers, revealing a Love beyond all we could imagine.

I am astonished by your generous invitation,
by your passionate urging,
for me to call on you.
In spite of my fears and uncertainties,
I am eager for contact.
And, so, I call to you.
Thank you that you hear me.
Thank you that you will respond
by showing me great and unsearchable things.

Prayer suggestion:

Sit quietly for a few minutes, reading and reflecting on the text from Jeremiah 33. With a humble, teachable spirit, allow yourself to seek conscious contact with God by simply calling on God. Stay open to whatever God may show you.

Saying Yes to God as Prayer

*Now choose life, so that you and your children may live
and that you may love the Lord your God, listen to his
voice, and hold fast to him. For the Lord is your life.*
Deuteronomy 30:19b-20a

Saying "no" to false gods can, perhaps, be compared to the
Israelites crossing the Red Sea, taking the first steps of leaving their life of slavery in Egypt. They were now moving toward
new freedom. Freedom to be all that God made them to be, and
to worship and serve God.

Saying "maybe" to the God of love and grace can, perhaps. be
compared to the Israelites living in the desert, freed from slavery
but uncertain and afraid in their relationship with God. God
feeds them and leads them and cares for them. God teaches
them more and more to trust that God is with them and loves
them.

Saying "yes" to God may be compared to entering the promised land. We have much to learn, we are still children spiritually, but our trust in God's love has grown. We are more often
able to open ourselves to God's love and take it in. We are more
often able to trust God's personal love and care.

To say "yes" to the God of love and grace is to say yes to Love.
We meditate, as the psalmist did, on "God's unfailing love." We
sit in the presence of this love. We receive this love. We let this
love heal us and fill us. The prayer of "yes" to God is the prayer
of taking in God's love and of opening our hearts to return that
love.

In saying "yes" to the God of love we are also listening to
God's voice of wisdom and guidance for us each day. The prayer
of "yes" is the prayer of surrender. It is the prayer of the sheep

who knows the Shepherd's voice and follows the Shepherd's lead.

In saying "yes" we are "holding fast" to God, even while God "holds fast" to us. The prayer of "yes" to God is the prayer of acknowledgment that God is our most intimate other. The prayer of "yes" to God is the prayer of engaging in an intimate, loving, joyful relationship with the One who made us, the One who longs for closeness with us and the One for whom our soul longs.

We will continue to have times when we doubt God's love and personal care. There will be times when we hesitate to follow our Shepherd's lead. There will be times when we resist the intimacy we desire. But once we have entered this promised land and tasted the milk and honey, we will find ourselves asking for the grace to say "yes" again and again.

Today I say yes to you, God.
I say yes to your love for me.
May I receive your love.
May I rest in your love.
I say yes as well to your
loving will for me.
I say yes to all you would
teach me and change in me.
I say yes to you, my Love, my Life.

Prayer suggestion:

As you sit quietly, notice both your readiness and your resistance to saying "yes" to God's love for you. Notice as well your readiness and your resistance to saying "yes" to God's loving will for you. As you can, ask for the grace to say "yes". As you can, say "yes" to the God of love.

Awakening as Prayer

Awake my soul!
awake, harp and lyre!
I will awaken the dawn.
I will praise you, O Lord, among the nations;
I will sing of you among the peoples.
For great is your love, reaching the heavens;
your faithfulness reaches the skies.
Psalm 57:8-10

Prayer is awakening. We have a tendency to fall asleep spiritually. Too often we forget who we are and what life is about. We forget the deeper realities of our existence. We fall asleep.

Prayer wakes us up. The act of prayer is an acknowledgment of our spiritual nature. It is an acknowledgment of our longing for relationship with God. It reminds us that there is more to life than what we see and touch. It reminds us that there is more to life than the pressures we face and the distractions we chase after. Prayer wakes us up to God's presence. It awakens us to the reality of the spiritual significance of ordinary life. It awakens us to the truth that life is an adventure that was meant to be lived in relationship with God.

But there is more. The awakening that prayer can bring has the potential of moving deeper and deeper into our hearts in a way that heals us and frees us from the depths of our stupor and forgetfulness.

Many of us have forgotten who God is. We have forgotten that God is love and that God's love for us is intimate and unconditional. And many of us have forgotten who we are and who others are. We have forgotten that we are all God's beloved children.

We may have come to believe that the opposite is true. We may have come to believe that God is harsh, punitive or abandoning. And we may have come to believe that we, or our neighbor, are unlovable. But this is not who God is. This is not who we are. And it is not who our neighbor is.

As we open our hearts and minds to God's loving Spirit, these lies about God, about ourselves and about our neighbors can begin to fade. We can begin to awaken to the reality of who God is and to who we are and to who our neighbor is.

In prayer we are invited to awaken more and more to the reality of God's love and to awaken more and more to the reality that we, along with all others, are loved. This is an awakening in joy and freedom, to be our true selves, to honor the dignity of each human being and to rest and rejoice in God's unfailing love for us. This is the deepest awakening of all.

Prayer is learning to sing with the psalmist, " Awake my soul! awake, harp and lyre! I will awaken the dawn. I will praise you, O Lord, ...for great is your love, reaching the heavens; your faithfulness reaches the skies."

Thank you for waking me up.
Thank you that prayer invites us
to the deepest awakening of all,
to remember who you are
who we are
and who our neighbor is.
Thank you for your unfailing love.
Thank you that we are your
beloved children.
Your love is so great, so vast,
so faithful!
Thank you for waking me
from my fearful slumber
into the glorious truth
of who you are.

Prayer suggestion:

Celebrate the awakenings that prayer has brought into your life.

Ask God to show you what further awakenings God might have for you.

Communing with God as Prayer

I will praise the Lord, who counsels me,
even at night my heart instructs me,
I have set the Lord always before me.
Because he is at my right hand,
I will not be shaken.

Psalm 16:7-8

We are invited to engage with God in ongoing conversation. Night and day we listen as God counsels and instructs us. Night and day we practice awareness of God's loving, guiding presence. Night and day we commune with God.

The prayer of communion with God is the prayer of praying "without ceasing". It is the prayer of the "practice of the presence" that Brother Lawrence described when he said that it did not matter if he was kneeling in prayer in the chapel or washing dishes in the kitchen, he was engaged in the prayer of communion with God.

We may not think that such a prayer is real. We may think it is just for those who are in full time religious work of some kind. But this kind of prayer is real. And it is meant for everyone. It is the expression of the deepest truth about prayer—that it is a relationship with God. It is an ongoing, vital, personal, communicating, communing relationship with the living God.

Thomas Kelly says this about the prayer of communion:

> Deep within us all there is an amazing inner sanctuary of the soul, a holy place, a Divine Center, a speaking Voice, to which we may continuously return. Eternity is in our hearts, pressing upon our time-torn lives, warming us with intimations of an astounding destiny, calling us home unto

Itself. Yielding to these persuasions, gladly committing ourselves in body and soul, utterly and completely, to the Light Within, is the beginning of true life....How, then, shall we lay hold of that Life and Power, and live the life of prayer without ceasing? By quiet, persistent practice in turning all our being, day and night, in prayer and inward worship and surrender, toward Him who calls in the deeps for our souls....One can live in a well nigh continuous state of unworded prayer, directed toward God, directed toward people and enterprises we have on our heart. (Thomas Kelly *A Testament of Devotion*, 1941, Harper Collins New York, New York, pages 3, 11, 98)

The prayer of communion with God is a way of life in which God becomes our most intimate Other. God is the Light within us and around us. God is our Breath, our Hope, our Wisdom, our Life. We talk to God about everything. We consult with God about everything. We listen to God's counsel. We find strength in God's constant presence with us. We return again and again throughout each day and night to our heart's true Home.

You are my Life.
You are the Light within me.
You are my Guide,
my Joy,
my closest Friend.
Thank you that you counsel me.
Thank you for guiding me.
Awaken me each moment
to awareness of you.
May I live a life of
communion with you.

Prayer suggestion:

Begin to practice turning your heart and mind toward God throughout the day and any time at night that you are awake. You might find it helpful to gently move your focus from your head to your heart, even placing your hand over your heart, remembering the "amazing inner sanctuary of the soul—the Divine Center" within. Continue this practice every day, asking God to help you live in awareness of God's loving voice and presence with you.

Living in God's Presence as Prayer

*The God who made the world and everything in it is the
Lord of heaven and earth and does not live in temples
built by human hands. And he is not served by human
hands, as if he needed anything. Rather, he himself gives
everyone life and breath and everything else....He is not
far from each one of us. For in him we live and move and
have our being.*
Acts 17:24-25, 27-29

Prayer is living with the awareness that God is near—that
God is all around us and within us. Prayer is looking and
listening for God's loving, life-giving presence everywhere we
go, in all circumstances. Prayer is trusting that the faintest whisper, the quietest thought or deepest longings of our heart are all
known to God.

Sometimes it can feel as if God is far away. This experience of
God as distant can have deep roots in our lives. We may have
experienced distance and abandonment from some of the most
important people in our lives and, as a result, fear a similar kind
of distance and abandonment from God. We may fear that we
are not good enough, that we are not measuring up in some
way and that God is distant and disapproving of us. Or we may
simply be emotionally or physically spent, too exhausted to
sense any emotional connection with ourselves or with others,
including God.

Even though all of these things which make it difficult for us
to experience God's presence, the sense of God's distance is an
illusion. God is with us. Always.

This text from the books of Acts is a portion of a speech that
the Apostle Paul gave in Athens to a population that worshipped idols made of sliver and gold. Their gods were small

and demanding. Paul is challenging their vision of God. He is expanding their understanding. Paul is speaking of a God who is vast in power as Creator and Sustainer of all. He speaks of "the God who made the world and everything in it, the Lord of heaven and earth". Paul goes on to say that God is not served by human hands, but is the One who gives breath and life to all. This God, Paul tells his audience, desires that we would "reach out and find him, though he is not far from each of us."

We do not have to worship idols carved from silver and gold to engage in idol worship. Our private fears about God diminish God. We carve idols in our imaginations, gods that are small and demanding, sometimes without even being aware of what we are doing.

Prayer calls us back to the vision of God that Paul shared with the people of Athens. The vision of God as the Creator and Sustainer of all, the One who gives us breath, longs for relationship with us and is physically and emotionally close to us.

I wrote about the perception of God's closeness in a previous book entitled *Keep Breathing*. Here is one story from that book that captures my own experience of what is near and what is at a distance:

> Some mornings when I am out walking I look up at the sky and it seems far away. On other days I realize that the sky kisses the earth. As I walk, I move through sky. I walk surrounded by sky. I breathe in the sky. It lives inside of me. Whether the sky seems close or far away, the truth is that it is always close. And, so with God. God is the One in whom we "live and breathe and have our being." God is with us. Always. God's loving presence caresses us, surrounds us, fills us. (Juanita Ryan, *Keep Breathing*. CreateSpace, 2009. pg. 116)

Prayer is living in awareness of this truth.

Sometimes I diminish you
in my fearful imagination.
I think of you as distant
and uncaring.
Help me to live in awareness
of who you are,
Creator, Sustainer of all,
God with us.
Allow me the prayer
of living in awareness
of your intimate presence,
your desire for relationship,
your loving closeness.

Prayer suggestion:

In a time of quiet ask God to give you eyes to see the Divine Presence with you, around you and within you.

Sit for a time with this awareness.

Ask God to help you to live more and more in conscious contact with your Creator..

Living in the Present as Prayer

Look at the birds of the air; they do not sow or reap or store away in barns, and yet your heavenly Father feeds them. Are you not much more valuable than they? Who of you by worrying can add a single hour to his life?...Therefore do not worry about tomorrow...
Matthew 6:26. 27.34

Many of us find that it is all too easy to get lost in the maze of our minds. We do this without even realizing it. We may be thinking about something in the future, or obsessing about some problem or reviewing some event in the past. Often this is not particularly valuable or productive thinking. In fact, it tends to be counter-productive because it distracts us from whatever it is that is right in front of us that needs our attention.

It may distract us from an activity we are engaged in, or, even worse, this kind of mental spinning may distract us from the person we are with. It also disrupts the restfulness or peacefulness we might otherwise enjoy if we were allowing ourselves to simply be present in the moment.

But there is an even deeper problem with this kind of mental spinning. The distraction and unnecessary noise created by mentally being somewhere else other than the present robs us from being present to God. It robs us from being present to God who is always present to us.

God is the Giver of life and of all good things. God is with us in each moment, moment by moment. But too often we are elsewhere, in our minds, missing this, the greatest gift of all.

When we are spinning and distracted about something it can be helpful to offer a simple prayer about our concern. "Lord show me what to do." Or perhaps, "Lord, thank you that you will show me what to do. You will guide me." These simple prayers, can release us from unproductive mental spinning. Our mind and body will relax a bit and we will find that we are able to rest in the moment. Our heart and mind can now be freed to listen to the Spirit's wisdom and guidance.

Another way of praying that can help us practice living in the present is to pray, as often as we can remember during the day, "Lord, allow me to be present to (whatever it is I am engaged with at the moment), and to you." For example, we might pray, "Lord, allow me to be present to driving to work and to you." Or, "Lord, allow me to be present to making this meal and to you."

Whatever it is that we are engaged in at the moment, no matter how ordinary, takes on new joy and wonder as we pray this way. When we pray in this way we are reminded of the reality of God's presence with us. And we are brought back to the gift of the present moment. One moment at a time.

"Don't worry about tomorrow," Jesus tells us. "Look at the birds of the air, they do not sow or reap or store away in barns, and yet your heavenly Father feeds them." God will take care of us. God will guide and provide for us. Our work is to live in the present so we can receive the gift of God's loving care one moment at a time.

Help me to live in the present.
Allow me to be present to you,
as you are always present to me,
each moment of each day.
Allow me to be present
to the gift of each moment,
no matter how ordinary,
so that I can be present
to the joy
and wonder
of your loving presence
each moment of each day.

Prayer suggestion:

As you remember throughout the day, pray, "God allow me to be present to (whatever you are doing in the moment) and to you."

Prayer as Being Loved by God

When we respond to God's call to us and acknowledge our Maker—to whatever degree we are able, in what ever way we can—we enter the dance. What we may not know is that the One who made us has been singing songs of love and joy over us all our lives. Long before we began to respond, God was loving us. God has been singing for joy over us. Our Maker has been holding us, blessing us, pouring out grace and love to us, always.

Love is what our hearts ache for. And love is ours. It is built into the foundation of everything. We are loved by God with a love that is faithful, sure, unconditional, patient, merciful, forgiving, joyful, unshakable. This is the good news of the Christian story. This is what Jesus came to show us, tell us, live out for us, pour out for us.

Intellectually we see this. We acknowledge a God of love. But we are wounded, sometimes early and deeply, in our ability to live as if this were true. We don't trust that we are loved. We don't trust that we are valued. We fall prey to fears that we have to earn love or prove ourselves worthy of love.

These wounds cause us to guard our hearts. They cause us to resist the thing we were made for and long for. They cause us to keep a distance in our dance with God.

To heal, to be whole, to know the fullness of life we need to breathe in deeply this Love that is ours. We need to open our hearts to take in this love. We need to rest in this Love. We need to live in this Love so that this Love can live in us.

Prayer is this: it is being loved by God. It is allowing ourselves to take in the love that is ours in God.

Hearing God's Love Songs as Prayer

The Lord your God is with you,
he is mighty to save.
He will take great delight in you,
he will quiet you with his love,
he will rejoice over you with singing.
Zephaniah 3:17

Prayer is taking in God's delight in us. Prayer is being quieted by God's love. Prayer is listening to God sing songs of joy over us.

Whether our parents delighted over us or not, whether our parents quieted us with love or not, whether our parents sang for joy about us or not, God does.

God delights in us. God loves us. God is singing songs about us. God is rejoicing over us with singing.

Prayer is allowing ourselves to hear those songs of love and joy.

Most of us probably have never imagined that such pure, joyful love could be directed toward us. Many of us see ourselves as unlovable or as worthless. And many of us see God as disappointed in us, or as rejecting of us.

So the thought of God singing love songs to us and songs of joy about us may be more than we can take in. We may read these words and find that they do not penetrate our minds or hearts. They may fall on hardened soil. Our fears, shame, guilt and despair may keep us from hearing God singing over us. As a result, we may feel incapable of participating in the prayer of listening to God's songs of love for us.

Try for just a moment to imagine what it might be like to pray in this way. Imagine what it would be like to ask God to open your heart, mind and spirit to listen for God's songs of love and joy. Imagine what it would be like to see God as One who delights in you and loves you this tenderly and powerfully. Imagine what it might be like to see yourself as loved and cherished in this way by your Maker.

The truth is that if we allowed ourselves to listen to God's songs it would transform our lives. The sweetness and the power of God's songs of love would begin to turn our fear into security, our shame into childlike humility, our guilt into release, our despair into hope.

We would begin to experience God in new ways. We would experience God as the One who looks at us through eyes of love. We would come to know God as the kind and loving parent we have always longed for God to be. And we would begin to know ourselves in new ways. We would know ourselves as loved and lovable, as cherished and of infinite value to the One who made us.

Prayer is hearing the songs of love that God is singing over us.

Help me to hear your songs
of love and joy and delight.
Help me to begin to believe
that these songs you sing
are for me.
May I take in the comfort
of your love.
May your love quiet my fears
and shame and despair.
May I hear the songs of joy
you sing over me.
May your songs heal
how I see you,
how I see myself,
how I see all others.

Prayer suggestion:

Ask God to quiet and comfort your anxious thoughts.

Ask God to help you hear the songs of joy God is singing over you.

Allow yourself to sit quietly and listen, as you are able, to God's love songs.

If this feels impossible, let it be. The time will come when the music will break through for you to hear.

Being Held as Prayer

If I rise on the wings of the dawn,
if I settle on the far side of the sea,
even there your hand will guide me,
your right hand will hold me fast.
Psalm 139:9-10

Prayer is knowing that wherever we go, wherever we are, we are held securely by God. We might pray this way by reflecting on images of being held by Love. We might sit quietly for a few minutes and feel ourselves held securely in God's hand, or experience ourselves as children in the arms of Jesus, or allow ourselves to feel the protective embrace of being surrounded by the light of God's presence.

But we do not need to limit our experience of praying in this way to moments of quiet. The images and sensations of being held by God's loving hand, or in the safe and tender arms of Jesus, or embraced by God's light, can continue with us as we go about our day. We can carry these realities with us. Or allow them to carry us.

We do well to live there. Protected in God's hand. Comforted in those arms. Resting in that Presence. We can continue to drink in love. We can continue to receive deep comfort. We can continue to find refuge there throughout the day and the night.

This is the deepest truth, the surest reality—we are all held in the loving arms and hands of God. As the psalmist wrote, "God's hand guides us, God's hand holds us fast".

Prayer is being aware that we are held. It is allowing ourselves to live there, to rest there, to find our security there. Wherever we are, wherever we go, if we "rise on the wings of the dawn or settle on the far side of the sea," we are held in God's caring hands.

In describing what it might mean to be held in God's loving hands, Richard Foster in his book, *Prayer*, offers an image of how a person might hold a wounded bird with cupped hands.

"For us, too, the hands of God are cupped lightly. We have enough freedom so that we can stretch and grow, but also we have enough protection so that we will not be injured— so we can be healed." (Richard Foster, *Prayer*, Harper San Francisco, 1992. Page 103)

We are held gently, respectfully, competently, constantly, securely. When we allow ourselves to be in those hands and relax there, we begin to heal. Our fears begin to ease. Our shame begins to diminish. We experience ourselves less as a separate being, alone in a dangerous world, and more as a person who is a part of a family. We experience ourselves as one of God's much loved children.

You hold me.

You hold me gently, letting me be a child.

In your arms it is okay to not understand,

It is acceptable to say "it is too hard for me."

I can say "I need you,"

I can say it all the time.

You hold me securely, letting me be a child.

Making it safe to love you—

sweet innocence restored,

helping me to feel

myself tenderly loved by You.

You hold me always, letting me be a child.

Letting me be alive, playful, stilled, quieted.

Letting me rest knowing, in your arms, all is well.

Prayer suggestion:

Choose an image of what it might mean for you to be held in love by God. Perhaps sitting with Jesus' arms around you or perhaps being a wounded bird held in God's cupped hands or surrounded by the light of God's presence. Or perhaps another image will come to you.

Sit quietly, breathing deeply and easily for a minute or two and let yourself be held by God in this way. Do not force this. If you sense fear or resistance simply pay attention to whatever your response is. To whatever extent you can, allow yourself to be held in love. Allow this truth to go with you throughout the day and night.

Being Blessed by God as Prayer

And he took the children in his arms,
put his hands on them and blessed them.
Mark 10:16

Sometimes prayer is receiving God's blessing. Sometimes prayer is allowing Jesus to gently place his hands on us and speak words of blessing over us.

To bless someone is to envision a positive future for them. It is to speak of the promise of God's care and provision throughout their lives.

We often envision the future in frightening ways. It is not always easy for us to think of the future as a place where God will meet us with grace, help and love. But God, in Jesus, stretches out his loving hands over us and speaks words of blessing and hope, showing us a future that is full of promise.

To bless someone is also to speak words of affirmation over them. It is to verbalize belief in the person being blessed. It is to say specifically what one sees that is good and hopeful in the person.

Too often we see ourselves through eyes of shame and judgement or, in an attempt to defend against this pain, we may see ourselves through grandiose lenses. God's blessing is an antidote both to our negative self assessments and to our grandiose defenses. God's blessing over us is a reminder that we are loved, that we can rest in the presence of the One who made us and sustains us.

Rachel Remen, in her book *My Grandfather's Blessings*, wrote about how her grandfather would bless her with words of affirmation every week:

My grandfather would set two candles on the table and light them. Then he would have a word with God in Hebrew....When Grandpa finished talking to God, he would turn to me and say, 'Come, Neshume-le.' Then I would stand in front of him and he would rest his hands lightly on top of my head. He would begin by thanking God for me and for making him my grandpa. He would specifically mention my struggles during that week and tell God something about me that was true. Each week I would wait to find out what that was. If I had made mistakes during the week, he would mention my honesty in telling the truth...If I had taken even a short nap without my night light, he would celebrate my bravery in sleeping in the dark. (Rachel Remen, *My Grandfather's Blessings*, Riverhead Books, New York, 2000, pp 22-23.)

This story of Rachel's grandfather blessing her so specifically and intimately is a powerful picture of what God does for us. God blesses us. God speaks words of affirmation. God speaks to us about our infinite value. God shows us a future in which God is always with us, providing for us, helping us and empowering us to be all we were meant to be.

This is what God, in Jesus, did for the children. It is what Jesus opens his arms and heart to do for all of us.

You bless me.
I too often envision a future
that is frightening.
But you speak words
of promise and hope to me.
I often see myself through eyes of fear
as never good enough,
and at other times through grandiose lenses
as anything but your humble, dependent child.
But you speak words
of affirmation to me,
reminding me of your work in me,
reminding me of my growth in love and grace,
teaching me to be the much loved child I am.
You bless me, God.
Help me to receive your blessing.

Prayer suggestion:

Sit quietly. Allow yourself to be a child, standing in front of Jesus or in Jesus' arms. Listen for the words of hope and affirmation Jesus is speaking over you. Allow yourself to receive this blessing.

Christ Dwelling in Our Hearts as Prayer

*I pray that out of his glorious riches he may strengthen you
with power through the Spirit in your inner being, so that
Christ may dwell in your hearts through faith. And I pray
that you, being rooted and established in love, may have
power, together with all the saints, to grasp how wide and
long and high and deep is the love of Christ, and to know
this love that surpasses knowledge.*
Ephesians 3:16-19

Some of us may have had the experience as children of
responding to an invitation in Sunday School or church
to "pray to let Jesus come into your heart." In fact we may have
responded to many such invitations, sometimes out of uncertainty about whether or not earlier responses had "counted" and
sometimes out of a genuine longing for something more in our
relationship with God.

But according to this text from Ephesians, the Spirit has to
make us ready to receive the indwelling of love, the indwelling
of Christ. And this being made ready to "know this love that
surpasses knowledge" is an ongoing process.

The author of this text from Ephesians prays for those who
are followers of Christ to be "strengthened with power through
the Spirit in their inner being, so that Christ may dwell in their
hearts." What is being described here is an ongoing process of
being strengthened and transformed.

The text refers to the process of being empowered by the
Spirit in our inner being. And to the process of being "rooted
and established in love". These transformational processes can
make us people capable of experiencing the love of Christ
which is so "wide and long and high and deep" that it is beyond

our grasp. These processes are part of the on-going richness of encounters with the love and grace of God.

The more we encounter grace, the more we are rooted in love. The more we are strengthened in our inner being by a growing trust in the love of Christ, the more our hearts and spirits are made tender and open to the deep and abiding presence of Christ with us and in us.

Our spirits are joined by the Spirit of God and we are filled full of God, filled full with love. This is the meaning of Christ dwelling in our hearts. It is radical, humbling, glorious.

Prayer is asking that God would do this work in us. That God would make us ready to receive the love of Christ. That God would establish us in love. That God would allow us to grow in our experience of the love of Christ which surpasses knowledge. That our hearts and spirits would be opened and enlarged to know more and more deeply the presence of Christ with us and in us.

Strengthen me
in my inner being,
establish me in love,
allow me to know your love
truly, intimately,
your love that is beyond measure,
beyond knowing,
that my heart might be made tender
by your love,
that my spirit would be opened
and enlarged
to know your presence in me.
Live in me today.

Prayer suggestion:

Pray the prayer found in the Ephesians text for yourself, using your own words. Pray this prayer for others in your life.

Knowing Intimacy with God as Prayer

My beloved spoke, and said to me: "Rise up, my love, my
fair one, and come away. For lo. the winter is past, the
rain is over and gone. The flowers appear on the earth; the
time of singing has come, and the voice of the turtledove is
heard in our land...My beloved is mine and I am his.
Song of Solomon 2:10-12,16

Prayer is intimacy with God. Our Maker, our God, seeks intimacy with us. Intimacy grows in the soil of respectful relationships. Intimacy requires a sense of emotional and spiritual safety that is mutual between the parties involved. It is the sense of trust that one will be met with acceptance, grace and love that opens the possibility for an ever deepening transparency with each other.

The experience of intimacy is the experience of deeply knowing and of being deeply known. It is the experience of being emotionally and spiritually (and sometimes physically) naked and unashamed with each other. Intimacy is a mutual loving that is tender, strong and enduring.

This text from Scripture comes from a book of love poems. The Song of Solomon is a series of poems that express the longing, the passion, the tenderness of an intimate relationship. This book honors the beauty and vulnerability of human intimacy and offers a picture of the intimacy that is possible with God.

Intimacy with God becomes possible as we let go of our pretense, of our self-reliance, of our efforts to hide. It becomes possible as we become naked and unashamed before God.

But even in this, God takes the lead. God became vulnerable in Jesus. God, in Jesus, come to us as a baby, weak and dependent. God, in Jesus, lived and laughed and wept and was tempted. God, in Jesus, openly expressed longing and love for each and every one of us. God, in Jesus, was literally stripped naked before the world.

As we begin to experience the reality of God's vulnerable availability to us, we grow in our freedom to give ourselves to God. We learn more and more to surrender in love to the One who is Love.

This giving of oneself and one's heart to God, as a response to receiving the Self and heart of God, is the intimacy to which prayer leads. It is the intimacy of knowing ourselves to be God's beloved. And of knowing God as our true Beloved.

It is the pure joy of being able to hear God's tender voice calling to us, ""Rise up, my love, my fair one, and come away."

You are my Beloved
and I am yours.
You call me your love,
your fair one.
You give your self to me,
your heart to me.
I give my self,
my heart to you.
Loving you,
being loved by you
is true joy.

Prayer suggestion:

Taking a few slow, easy breaths. Let yourself sense the Light of God 's love surrounding you. Let yourself sense the tender, vulnerable love of God toward you. As you are able, let go of all pretense and be vulnerable with God. Share your heart with God. Let God share God's heart with you.

Encountering the Love of God in Jesus

As the Father has loved me, so have I loved you.
Now remain in my love.
John 15:9

We have all watched loving adults bend low or kneel down, making themselves small so they can be face-to-face with a child. Adults do this instinctively out of a desire to connect and be present to the child. Out of loving desire to relate to small ones, big people make themselves temporarily small.

Our Creator loves us in this way. Desiring to be face-to-face with us, longing to express love directly, seeking close relationship with us, God became small. This is the Christian story. God, coming to us as a baby, a child, a man. God coming to us in Jesus. The astonishing claim Jesus made was that if we have seen him, we have seen the Father. To encounter Jesus is to encounter the One who made and loves us all.

Jesus came to show us the love of the Father. But Jesus was not well received. People did not expect to see such love. Instead, they expected to see what we often expect to see in God. Rigidity. Harshness. Stern enforcement of the rules. Judgement. Distance. Rejection. Exclusion. Instead, in Jesus, they encountered radical love.

Jesus embodied God's incredible love—love that included the outcast, that honored women, that respected and blessed children, that embraced enemies, that touched and healed people with contagious diseases, that extended to prostitutes, that confronted abusive religious leaders, that valued loving relationships over rigid rule keeping, that made "heretics" the heros of his stories, that told stories of God-the-waiting-Father who runs like a servant to welcome us home and who sweeps like a woman to unearth us--her lost treasure.

This was a love that the religious powers could not tolerate. And so they plotted to kill Jesus. One way of seeing the story of Jesus' death, is that God's radical love was rejected by the religious authorities and by the people themselves. The love of God in Jesus which confronted the pride, hatred, greed and corruption of power of his day, simply by shining in the darkness, was put to death.

But another telling of this story is that in turning himself over to the powers of darkness that day, Jesus took this earth-shaking, heaven-rending love one step further. This Love gave itself completely. The Love of God in Jesus did not fight the power of violence with greater violence, but instead undid it with the one true Power in the universe. The power of darkness was undone by the Power of God's Love. In Jesus' death and resurrection we witness the powers of hate and evil being rendered powerless. We see that the Power of Love is what stands in the end. The Power of Love is always greater than the power of hatred and evil. The Light always overcomes the dark.

Prayer is God loving us with a love we struggle to comprehend and trust. When we pray we are allowing ourselves to be reshaped by a love that is beyond our wildest imaginations.

Prayer is being loved by God, with love that is respectful, patient, kind, faithful, full of hope, tender, intimate. And powerful! God's love is unshakable, enduring, never failing. It is powerful enough to create, heal, restore and make new.

Prayer is encountering the love of God in Jesus.

Maker of heaven and earth,
You stooped.
You bowed low.
You knelt.
You made yourself small like a parent with a child.
You came so close.
You came face-to-face
You came and showed us a love so wild and strong
that it surpasses knowledge or comprehension.
I marvel at this mystery.
Open my heart, my life,
to this Love beyond my wildest dreams.

Prayer suggestion:

In a time of quiet, ask God to help you to experience the Love expressed to us in Jesus. Sit in silence for ten minutes or more, breathing in this love. Notice whatever comes to your awareness. Continue to ask God to allow you to encounter the love as expressed to us in Jesus as you go through your day.

Prayer as Surrender

A time comes in our lives when we find ourselves at the end of ourselves. We hit a wall. We falter and fail. Things begin to crumble and we cannot seem to make them come right. We feel afraid, hopeless, undone.

It feels like a kind of death. We experience a grievous loss of our sense of ourselves.

What we usually don't realize is that it is necessary that we die to ourselves. It is in this death that grace is free to flow in new life giving ways.

We call out for help. Sometimes in spite of ourselves. Sometimes in despair. Sometimes in great fear.

We may have been in the dance with God for a long time. But perhaps we have been trying to be in the lead. Perhaps we have been trying hard to figure out the steps to get them "right". Or perhaps we have entered the dance and left, only to feel our need to return.

Our Beloved whispers to us, 'Let me lead. I am gentle and humble. And I know the dance. You can trust me to lead. You can relax in my arms. I will guide you through each step. I love you."

We are being invited into the prayer of surrender. This is the prayer of entrusting ourselves and all that holds our hearts into God's care. This is the prayer of living as if it is true—that we are loved by a Power far greater than ourselves who cares intimately for us. This is the prayer of dying so that we can begin to learn what it is to truly live.

Giving up Self-Reliance as Prayer

*Trust in the Lord with all your heart
and lean not on your own understanding;
in all your ways acknowledge him,
and he will make your paths straight.*
Proverbs 3:5-6

Prayer, by its nature, moves us away from our reliance on ourselves and towards reliance on God. This text from Proverbs instructs us in this basic wisdom. "Trust in the Lord," it says. Rely on God, lean on God, turn to God for wisdom, guidance and help.

The text goes on to tell us that as we lean on God we are to lean away from our own understanding. This does not mean that being people of faith requires us to check our brains at the door. It does mean that we remember that God is God and we are not. It means that we live with the reality of our limits. It means that we keep in mind how limited our understanding is, how limited our knowledge is, how limited we are in our ability to manage our lives on our own.

The image of leaning on God and the image of leaning on our own understanding represent two different paths for life. The path we are most familiar with is the path of trying to figure everything out, trying to get it all right. The well worn path is the path of relying on our own strength and understanding. The path of leaning on God—of trusting God with all our heart—is the path less traveled by most of us.

The wisdom of giving up self-reliance and learning to rely on God in all we do is counter intuitive for most of us. We have been taught to value self-reliance, to see it as the goal of human development. We have not been taught to value reliance on others, not even reliance on God.

Even within Christian circles, we have lost the core value and practice of reliance on God rather than reliance on ourselves. Prayer and Scripture reading and other religious practices have become activities we do as a kind of performance to win God's approval. These things that are meant to open our hearts to the love and wisdom of God become things we do in order to feel like we are doing all the right things and jumping through all the right hoops.

But prayer is not a performance to placate an angry or demanding God. Prayer is an acknowledgment of our need for God. Prayer is child-like trust in a loving God who desires to guide us and bless us.

All of Scripture tells us that life was meant to be lived, not in reliance on ourselves, but in full, joyful reliance on the One who made us and who is with us always. Life was meant to be lived in vital, intimate, daily turning to God in all we do, knowing our need of God and trusting that God will make clear the path before us.

According to the wisdom of this text from Proverbs, relying on God is a matter of the heart. We trust God with our whole heart. Relying on God rather than on ourselves means we give our heart to God, we give our love to God. We do this because God has already given God's heart to us. Because God loves us dearly we can entrust God with our hearts and with our lives.

You invite my full trust.

I do not have to know it all, understand it all, figure it all out.

I often strive to control things that are not in my control.

I try to figure out matters that are beyond understanding.

But I can let go of my attempts to be in charge.

I can let go of reliance on myself

and begin to rely on you instead.

You know, you see, you understand.

And you invite me to lean on you, to let you guide me.

Teach me to give up self-reliance.

Teach me to trust you with my whole heart

and to seek your guidance in all I do.

Prayer suggestion:

Talk to God about the fears that make it difficult for you to trust God with all your heart.

Talk to God about your desire to trust God with all your heart.

Ask God to increase your capacity for trust.

Ask God for help and guidance in all you do today.

Acknowledging our Need
of God's Provision as Prayer

Give us this day our daily bread.
Luke 11:3

Prayer is acknowledging our need of God's help. We tend to dislike our needs. We tend to want to meet our needs by ourselves. We may even feel ashamed of our needs. As a result, we are often afraid to rely on anyone else to help us, even God. But as we move away from self-reliance and begin to rely more and more on God, we begin to see how great our need is for God's love and care.

Many of the psalms clearly express the need for God's help and care. In Psalm 86, the writer begins by referring to himself as "poor and needy." (Psalm 86:1). He goes on to list his needs to God, trusting that God will respond with help and mercy, because he has come to trust that God is "forgiving and good, abounding in love...compassionate and gracious." (Psalm 86: 5, 15).

As we grow in our trust that God is loving and good, we are gradually freed from the fear and shame that keep us from turning to God with our needs. As we experience God's loving response to our needs, we come to trust that God always welcomes us and our needs.

The writer and theologian George MacDonald described God's relationship with us and our needs like this:

> God is infinitely more bound to provide for his child than any man is to provide for his. God created both the child and his hunger. The relation is infinitely, divinely closer. It is God to whom every hunger, every aspiration, every desire, every longing of our nature is to be referred. He made them

all—made us the creature of a thousand necessities—and have we no claim to him?...The child has, and must have, a claim on the Father, a claim which it is the joy of the Father's heart to acknowledge. A created need is a created claim. God is the origin of both need and supply, the Father of our necessities, the abundant giver of all good things." (George MacDonald, *Discovering the Character of God*. Compiled by Michael R. Phillips, Minneapolis: Bethany House Publishers 1989, pp. 206-07).

Because our needs are so important to God, when Jesus taught his disciples how to pray, part of what he taught them was how to pray about their needs. "Give us this day our daily bread," Jesus prayed.

Jesus' prayer of need begins with the phrase, "Give us." This phrase holds a lot of wisdom in its two simple words. The word "give" expresses our need for God and our willingness to turn to God with our need. It also expresses a trust that God is a Giver of good gifts, that God is for us and not against us, that God sees and responds to us and to our needs.

The word "us" assumes that whatever need we are experiencing is also a need that others are experiencing. It is an expression of our common humanity, of the brotherhood and sisterhood of the human race. Sometimes our needs can leave us self focused. We can forget the needs of others in the midst of our struggles. On the other hand, our needs can be a vehicle that brings us together in common concern and support for each other. The word "us" calls us out of our isolation and self focus, back to allowing ourselves to be cared for and to care for others, to be prayed for and to pray for others.

Jesus continued in his prayer of need with the phrase, "this day." Jesus teaches us here what he taught elsewhere, to be present to each day, one day at a time. We bring our needs to God each day, one day at a time. We tend to project our fears and worries into the future. Jesus reminds us not to live in the future, but to ask for and to look for God's love and care for us today.

Finally, Jesus' last phrase in this simple prayer of need is an expression of a specific need: "our daily bread." We are invited to ask God for specific help with our specific needs.

You see my needs.
You invite me to bring my needs to you.
I feel a lot of shame about my needs.
I try so hard to take care of myself, by myself.
But the truth is, I need you
We all need you.
We need your help and care today.

Prayer suggestion:

What is it like for you to acknowledge your need of God's help?

What help are you needing today?

Allow yourself to enlarge your focus to include the needs of those around you.

Talk to God about your need for God's help simply, directly, specifically.

Ask God to show you how you might be a part of God's care for others in need.

Entrusting All to God as Prayer

Therefore, I urge you...in view of God's mercy,
to offer your bodies as living sacrifices
holy and pleasing to God—
this is your spiritual act of worship.
Do not conform any longer to the pattern of this world,
but be transformed by the renewing of your mind.
Then you will be able to test and approve
what God's will is—his good, pleasing and perfect will.
Romans 12:1-2

Prayer is an act of entrusting ourselves and all that we care about to God's loving care. As David Benner, in his book *Surrender to Love*, puts it:

> The English word surrender carries the implication of putting one's full weight on someone or something. It involves letting go—a release of effort, tension and fear. And it involves trust. One cannot let go of self-dependence and transfer dependence to someone else without trust (David Benner, *Surrender to Love: Discovering the Heart of Christian Spirituality*, Downers Grove, Ill.: InterVarsity Press, 2003.)

According to this text from Romans, it is because of God's mercy that we can entrust ourselves to God. It is in view of God's tender, powerful, unshakeable love for us, that we can allow ourselves to relax into the ocean of God's love. Prayer, then, is a surrender to love. It is a laying down of our despair that we are unloveable. It is an opening of our closed hearts and clenched fists to the possibility of resting in God's mercy and love. It is the daily act of inviting the One who is love to heal us and guide us.

This experience of letting go and relaxing into God's love is

119

what our hearts most long for and what our hearts most resist. We resist it because it means letting go of trying to be in charge of our own lives. It means letting go of trying to earn God's approval, and everyone else's approval. It means allowing ourselves to move into the vulnerability of a trusting child.

For many of us, the capacity to trust that we are loved or that we are lovable has been deeply wounded. We may long to rest in God's love, but find ourselves unable to do so. This inability may add to our fear and shame. And it may serve to increase our futile attempts to fix ourselves spiritually.

We cannot make ourselves surrender. We cannot force ourselves to relax into God's loving arms. We cannot do this on our own power. But we can ask God to free us to live in full, joyful surrender to God's will for us each day.

This text from the book of Romans urges us to surrender all. Our bodies. Our minds. Our wills. The bodies that we instinctively try to protect. Our minds that give us a false sense of control. Our wills that guide our daily choices. All that we are, we are urged to offer as a loving gift to the One who loves us, the One who desires to provide for us, teach us, and lead us. May we learn the joy, the peace, of such full surrender.

Lover of my soul,
You give yourself to me
and ask that, in return, I give myself to you.
You urge me to rest
body, mind and spirit
in your loving arms.
You ask me to entrust all that I am
and all that I have into your care.
Teach me this sweet surrender
to your love.

Prayer suggestion:

Sit quietly, inviting God to help you give yourself to God.

First, give your body to God. Wait in quiet. Entrust your body to God's care. Ask the Spirit to show you whatever the Spirit might show you about what this might mean for you. Allow yourself to physically relax into God's loving care.

Next, give your mind to God. Wait in quiet. Entrust your mind to God's care. Ask the Spirit to show you whatever the Spirit chooses to show you about what this might mean. Allow yourself to mentally relax into God's loving care.

Finally, give your will to God. Wait in quiet. Entrust your will to God's care. Ask the Spirit to reveal whatever the Spirit might reveal about God's will for you right now. Allow your whole being to relax into God's loving care.

Becoming Like Little Children as Prayer

At that time the disciples came to Jesus and asked,
Who is the greatest in the kingdom of heaven?
He called a little child and had him stand among them.
And he said: I tell you the truth, unless you change and
become like little children,
you will never enter the kingdom of heaven.
Therefore, whoever humbles himself like this child
is the greatest in the kingdom of heaven.
Matthew 18:14

This story begins with Jesus' disciples asking him a pressing question. "How do we win the competition to gain favor with God? What do we need to do to prove ourselves as the best of the best with God?"

The disciples saw the spiritual life as an opportunity to compete with each other by trying hard, trying harder and trying their hardest to gain God's approval. They saw God's love as something for which they needed to strive. They saw themselves as unloved and therefore needing to prove themselves to God.

Jesus' response was to show them how far off the mark their question was. Jesus did not do this to shame them, but to free them from their fears and distortions about God and about themselves. In response to their question Jesus called a little child and said to his disciples, "Look at this child. This is who you are. This is all you need to be or do. Simply be who you are. Let yourself be the dearly loved child of God that you are."

Jesus was telling his disciples that the kingdom of God is not a competition. He was saying there is no such thing as being the greatest. Jesus was telling them to give up this way of thinking and being in the world. He was calling them to live in the freedom and humility of a child.

Prayer is being a humble child. Dependent, trusting, teachable, open to love, responsive to love. Children know they need help. Children know they need love. Children respond with joy and exuberant love when they are seen and heard and valued.

We are God's dearly loved children. We can let go of striving to win God's love and approval. We cannot win God's love because it is already ours. Always. Unconditionally. We can let go of competition, pride and pretense because the people we believe ourselves to be in competition with are also dearly loved by God.

We are invited to the freedom of the humility of children—the freedom to be loved and to respond in love to God and others. This humility, this freedom, is the heart of prayer.

.

Free me to be a child.
Free me to know myself
loved by you.
Free me of pride
and pretense.
Release me from all the futile and unnecessary attempts
to prove myself worthy of your love.
Let me know the humble prayer
of being your much loved child.

Prayer suggestion:

Sit quietly, breathing deeply and easily. Ask God to help
you experience yourself as a much loved child—held and safe
in God's loving presence. Notice whatever sense you have of
childlike wonder, joy, playfulness, creativity, affection or energy.
Notice, as well, any need for comfort or nurture that this little
one might be experiencing. Let your child self find comfort and
love in the arms of Jesus.

Dying as Prayer

I tell you the truth, unless a kernel of wheat
falls to the ground and dies,
it remains only a single seed.
But if it dies, it produces many seeds.
John 12:24

Prayer awakens us. Prayer is a source of conscious contact with the One who is Life itself. So how is it that prayer is also the experience of dying? What might it mean that prayer leads us to fall, like a kernel of wheat, into the ground and die? In what way do we die? In what way do we, like the seed come back to a life that is fuller, richer, multiplied?

When the seed falls into the ground and dies, the hardened outer crust, which protects the inner life of the seed, slowly softens and falls away. As this happens, the inner core of the seed is exposed. This inner core is where the true life of the seed lies hidden. The outer shell was nothing but a protective crust. And, until it dies, the true life hidden in the center of the seed cannot blossom.

This is the image Jesus used when calling us to experience the prayer of dying. Jesus was saying that it is our protective outer shell that needs to die. The part of us we sometimes call our false self needs to slowly soften and fall away.

Our false self is the self we present to the world. It may be an angry self, a compliant self, a happy self, an in-charge self, a rebellious self, a clown self, a hard working self, an addict self, an intellectual self, a religious self. Our false self can have a hundred faces.

This outer shell was formed, usually without our full awareness, to protect us from whatever wounds we experienced in life. Our wounds usually leave us with fears about ourselves and about life. Because we cannot tolerate the pain of living with these fears, we instinctively develop some kind of defense or protection in order to cope. The wounds we experience in life can leave us afraid that we are unloved, worthless. At the same time that this fear is developing, a protective strategy is born. We began to protect ourselves by trying to prove to the world and ourselves that we have value. Whatever form this protective outer shell takes on, it is a false self.

Over time our protective strategy, our false self, becomes more and more robust and resistant to change. We may begin to think that this protective outer shell is actually who we are. Or we may fear that the part of us that is full of fear and shame is who we really are.

It is this false self that has to fall, like a seed, into the ground and die. Every day. So that our true self can emerge. So that the beloved child of God that we really are can blossom.

This is the gift of the prayer of dying. Whatever is false, whatever is prideful, whatever is self reliant, whatever is defensive, whatever is not real, needs to die, so that who we really are can live and produce more life.

You call me to die.

You invite me to let go of all that is false,
all that is prideful.

all that is an attempt to prove something,
all that is driven by fear,
all that is defensive.

It feels like a death.

Who will I be if I don't have my defenses?

Will I exist at all?

Today I give myself to this prayer of dying.

May all that is false and hard and proud in me die today.

May the fears that are exposed as this protective shield falls away
be healed by you.

May the kernel of true life that you created in me, lie exposed and
vulnerable.

May the naked seed of my true self
take root in the soil of your love
and blossom into fullness of life.

Prayer suggestion:

Ask God to reveal to you what needs to die in your life. Ask God to show you whatever is false or defensive. Ask God for the willingness to pray the prayer of dying.

Allow yourself to see the image given to us by Jesus: let yourself be the seed falling into the rich soil of God's love. Feel yourself held and surrounded by God's love. See the outer shell of your false self softening and falling away.

Receiving the Fullness of God as Prayer

*I pray that you, being rooted and established in love, may
have power... to grasp how wide and long and high and
deep is the love of Christ, and to know this love that surpasses knowledge—that you may be filled to the measure
of all the fullness of God.*
Ephesians 3: 17-19

As we fall like a seed into the ground and die to our self-reliance and self-serving ways, the true life God created in us
is exposed. This tender, vibrant life within us finds itself resting
in the vast, rich soil of God's love.

Slowly, we send out roots. Gradually we take in the nourishment of God. We feed on the kindness, the mercy, the
patience, the life that is God. Over time our spirit—our true
life within—becomes rooted in God. We become grounded in
Love itself.

God feeds us, nourishes us. God fills us to all fullness with
love, with God. Filled full of God. Filled with a love that is so
vast that it surpasses knowledge. This is an astounding proposi-
tion. It puts our minds on overload. We want to read past these
words because it doesn't seem like it could be real. But the true
life that God created in us stirs at these words. Our longing for
this love, for this One, moves within us. "Yes," something says
inside of us, "this is true, this is real, this is what I hunger for."

Prayer is saying "yes" to being "filled to the measure of all the
fullness of God." God's Spirit awakens and fills our spirits with
God's life and love. Prayer is receiving this gift. It is knowing—
intimately experiencing—"this love that surpasses knowledge."

The result of saying "yes" to the life of the Spirit being poured
into us is that the love of God begins to pour out of our lives as

well. The "love, joy, peace, patience, kindness, goodness, faithfulness, gentleness and self control" of the Spirit fill us and flow through us (Galatians 5:22-23). This miracle of grace is not our doing. This is God's doing. Our part is to consent. Our work is to ask for the willingness to let go of our way and to surrender to God's loving activity.

It is God's desire for us to fully grasp the scale of God's Love. It is God's desire that we "know this love that surpasses knowledge." It is God's desire to "fill us to the measure of all the fullness of God".

Prayer is responding with awed consent to God's loving, breath-taking desire to fill us to all fullness with God, with Love.

I am a seed
fallen into the ground,
releasing my outer shell to you.
All that is protective and false in me,
I give to you.
All that is real and true in me,
I give to you as well.
May the rich soil of your love nourish me
as I put out new roots.
Let me grow in the soil of your love.
Fill me with your life,
your goodness,
your love.

Prayer suggestion:

In a time of quiet see yourself, having fallen like a seed into the ground.

The tender life within is exposed.

You find yourself held and resting in the vast, rich soil of God's love.

See yourself putting out roots.

Feel yourself being fed and filled with love, with God.

As you are ready, say 'yes' to God's offer to fill you to all fullness with God's love.

Prayer as Honesty and Humility

Our resistance to God's loving initiative is rooted, in part, in our pride and self-reliance and in our attachments to a false sense of who we are.

We are each created in love by Love. God's intention is for us to know that we are loved. God's desire for us is that we live in loving relationship both with God and with each other. But we are wounded and confused. We have lost sight of who God is and who we are. We fear that it cannot possibly be true that we are unconditionally loved and valued by our Maker.

So we unknowingly set out to earn our worth. In the process we develop attachments to a false sense of ourselves. Instead of knowing ourselves to be the loved children of God that we are, we strive to show how smart we are, how spiritual we are, how attractive we are, how successful we are, how right we are, how cunning we are, how funny we are, how good we are, how cool we are, how superior we are, how in control we are. As a result, we become defended, guarded, protected. We hide behind a facade. We invest our hopes in our efforts to prove ourselves worthy. We become proud and dishonest and unable to engage in truly loving relationships.

Scripture tells us that we all sin, that we all miss the mark, that we all fall short of God's glory (Romans 3:23). The thought that we fall short of God's glory is remarkable. How could we be expected not to fall short of this glory? Can it be that this text is telling us in yet another way that God's glory is in us? That the light and love of our Maker, the beauty of who God is, is in us and that we have hidden it behind our self-will and pride?

In order for God's love and goodness to shine in us, we need to let go of our defensive ways. It means we have to let go of trying to earn the love and valuing that are already ours. It means we need to let go of our pride and attempts to look good. Instead we need to practice honesty and humility so that the glory of God's love that is in us can shine through us.

Honesty. And humility. These are not easy to come by. Even this we cannot do without God's grace and help.

But with God's grace and help we can begin to see and acknowledge that we are spiritually ill and need God's help, that we have been hurting others with our pride and pretense, that we need to let go of all that is false about us and learn a new way of living that is more loving and reflective of God's glory.

All of this is a vital part of prayer. Honest, humble living and praying frees us to begin to be who we are and to live the life of love we were created to enjoy.

Going to the Doctor as Prayer

*While Jesus was having dinner at Matthew's house, many
tax collectors and "sinners" came and ate with him and his
disciples. When the Pharisees saw this, they asked his disciples, "Why does your teacher eat with tax collectors and
"sinners"? On hearing this, Jesus said, "It is not the healthy
who need a doctor, but the sick. But go and learn what this
means: 'I desire mercy, not sacrifice. For I have not come to
call the righteous, but sinners."*
Matthew 9:10-13

Prayer is going to the Great Physician and admitting that we
are not well. The reality of our soul sickness is not an easy
thing for us to fully admit. We may know the truth about our
soul sickness only in an abstract way. The full reality of it may
be more than we can face. Instead of facing our soul sickness we
may keep ourselves busy trying to look good. We may work hard
at being righteous. We may desperately try to convince ourselves
and others that we are spiritually healthy.

In some ways it can come as a relief when this facade begins to
crumble. As distressing as it is to see our soul sickness, it can be a
relief to heed what Jesus says in this text. It can be a relief to stop
pretending to be spiritually healthy and to allow ourselves to fall
into God's merciful, healing hands.

The religious leaders and teachers to whom Jesus was speaking
in this passage were much like us. They were working hard to be
the best. They were striving to be perfect spiritually. They saw
themselves as spiritually healthy.

But, like us all, they were sick. They were sick with fear and
shame that they hid from themselves and others. They were sick
with guilt and dishonesty. They were sick with pride and greed.
They were sick with self-serving and self-reliance. They were sick

with defensiveness, with resentments, with judgments. They were so spiritually sick that they judged Jesus for showing mercy and grace to others. They were so spiritually sick that they did not see that they were in need of God's healing mercy.

Prayer is letting this exhausting facade of spiritual self righteousness crumble. Prayer is admitting that we are sick and in need of a doctor.

Prayer allows us to stop trying harder and harder to heal ourselves. Prayer is entrusting ourselves to the great mercy of God, the Healer.

Like any good physician it is God's desire for us that we acknowledge our sickness, not to shame us or judge us, but to begin a process of treatments that will lead to our healing and freedom. Prayer is going to the doctor so that the doctor can help us get well.

I have been working hard to convince myself
and others that I am spiritually healthy.
I have been proud
of how good I am,
of how righteous I am,
and even of how humble I can be.
This facade is crumbling.
I am experiencing the reality of my soul sickness.
I see how my self-reliance, my judgments and
my religious pride has hurt me and hurt others.
I see how it keeps me and those I judge from
your great mercy.
I am in need of your healing mercy.
I am in need of a physician.
I cannot heal myself.
Heal me, make me whole.

Prayer suggestion:

In a time of quiet reflection, ask God to show you the symptoms of your soul sickness.

Take some time to acknowledge your need for God to be your Physician.

Ask God to help you to entrust yourself to God's mercies and healing powers.

Honesty as Prayer

Have mercy on me, O God,
according to your unfailing love;
according to your great compassion
blot out my transgressions.
Surely you desire truth in the inner parts;
you teach me wisdom in the inmost place.
Psalm 51: 1,6

Prayer is not a performance. It is not an attempt to impress God. Prayer is honest communication. Transparency is the cornerstone of intimacy in any relationship, including our relationship with God.

In the story of Adam and Eve we see our instinctive response to failure. Adam and Eve failed and then they hid from God. They had been intimate with God, but now they were in hiding. "Where are you?" God called. God still calls us today. "Where are you? Come out of hiding, be honest with Me, it is the only way we can experience intimacy."

Honesty is the choice to come out of hiding.

Being honest means that we tell the truth about ourselves. It means we do not deny or minimize or blame. Instead, we acknowledge the truth about our thoughts, our feelings, our actions. This may sound easy, but it is often anything but easy. Honesty exposes our weaknesses, our needs, our fears, our failings. The truth about ourselves may feel shameful. We may be working so hard to defend ourselves against feelings of shame that we find it difficult to be honest. We may fear that God and others close to us will reject us if we tell the truth.

But if we think about how we might respond to a friend who is honest and transparent with us, we know that we would feel drawn to this friend, we would feel closer to them and we would be grateful for their trusting disclosure.

Our response to honesty in others is usually gratitude, appreciation, even tenderness. And so it is with God. God welcomes our honesty. God invites us to courageously practice "truth in the inner parts," trusting that God will respond to our honesty with compassion.

The psalmist begins this psalm by reflecting on God's unfailing love and compassion. When we feel safe with someone, we find it easier to be honest. When we trust that we are loved unconditionally, we are better able to expose our souls. Prayer is honesty with God. Prayer is revealing our souls to the One who loves us without fail.

Your mercy.

Your love.

Your compassion.

They are my hope.

They draw me out of hiding.

They call me to a place of transparency.

I come out of hiding with all my weaknesses and fears.

My 'inmost places' are not accustomed to the light of your Love.

Teach me to practice truth in my inmost being.

Teach me the wisdom of honesty where it matters the most.

Heal me.

Transform me.

May I be a person who no longer has a need to hide.

Make me a person whose insides are full of truth and wisdom.

Prayer suggestion:

Ask God to show you how you might be hiding from God.

Hear God calling to you, "Where are you?"

Ask God to help you to come out of hiding and to practice honesty with God.

Taking Inventory as Prayer

Search me, O God, and know my heart;
test me and know my anxious thoughts.
See if there is any offensive way in me,
and lead me in the way everlasting.
Psalm 139:23-24

We are often blind to our own failings. We do not see our prideful motives or greedy ways. We do not understand how our choices and behaviors are hurting others. We may not even be aware of the fears and anxieties that drive us and hold us captive. If anything is to change, we will need help to know ourselves better. We need God's help in order to take regular inventory of our lives.

And so we pray as the psalmist prayed. We ask God to help us take inventory of our lives. And with God's help, we make an honest assessment of our anxieties and of our offensive ways.

Usually when a conflict surfaces in a relationship our instinct is to reflect on the ways the other person needs to change. But when we catch ourselves and pray, "God show me what my part is in this conflict. How am I contributing to this problem? What do I need to do differently?" we inevitably will be shown places we need to change.

As God responds to our prayer to search us and show us, we begin to see our self-serving motives. We are given new awareness of the anxious thoughts that kept us defensive in the situation. We begin to understand the road blocks we put up to being truthful, respectful and loving toward others. When we ask for this kind of help, as the psalmist did, God's Spirit shows us our selfish hearts, our fears and anxieties, our offensive ways.

It can be helpful to write down what we sense God is showing us. And to then ask for God's help to change. We can ask God to free us from the self-centeredness, the fears and anxieties, the defensiveness and offensiveness that the Spirit has revealed to us.

There are many other ways to take inventory. Just to take one example, the Oxford Group movement in the early 1900's advocated making a regular written inventory by dividing a piece of blank paper into four sections. In one section we ask God to show us where we have been less than absolutely loving. In another section we ask God to show us where we have been less than absolutely pure. In a third section we ask God to show us where we have been less than absolutely honest. And in the fourth section we ask God to show us where we have been less than absolutely unselfish. Then we wait quietly and write down whatever comes to our minds.

However we take inventory, we need to do it with God's help. That is, we need to do it as the psalmist did, as an act of prayer. It is good to ask for God's loving correction in our lives on a daily basis. It will be painful to see the error of our ways. But the practice of inventory takes us to a place where God's grace can meet us. It is a place where it is possible to experience God's unconditional love and forgiveness.

I am in the dark.

I am blind to my own selfishness and greed.

I do not see my pride and defensiveness.

I am anxious but I deny even my anxiety.

Show me the error of my ways.

Show me where I need to change.

Show me where you would correct me and heal me.

Help me to take inventory.

Lead me in your way.

Prayer suggestion:

Use the words of the psalmist to ask God to show you your heart, your anxieties, your offensive ways and to lead you in the way of life. Wait quietly. Write down whatever you are sensing.

Try using the Oxford Group method of asking God to show you where you have been less than absolutely loving, pure, honest and unselfish. Wait quietly in prayer. Write down whatever comes to mind.

Confession as Prayer

I said, O Lord, have mercy on me;
heal me, for I have sinned against you.
Psalm 41:4

Prayer is sometimes confession. It is the acknowledgment of our short comings, our missing the mark, our moral failings. Confession is also the acknowledgment of our longing to change, our longing to be healed and our longing to be set free to love God and others.

When we confess to God, we throw ourselves on God's mercy. It is, in fact, because of God's mercy that we can come to God with our confession and our need for healing.

Many of us imagine that God will not respond with mercy. We imagine that God is disappointed with us, angry with us, waiting to punish us. We may imagine that we have to clean up our act before we can come to God. All of this leaves us believing that we are on our own to somehow do the good we long to do, but cannot seem to do.

But we are not on our own. We do not have to clean up our mess before we come to God. Like the psalmist, we can come to God in the middle of the mess we have made and throw ourselves on God's love and mercy. We can run to God and acknowledge our sin and our need for help and healing.

God is our loving parent. And, like a loving parent, God welcomes our confession and our desire to live a life of love. Imagine a parent whose child confesses that they said something mean to a friend at school. Imagine the child asking for help to learn to not be so angry and mean to this friend. A loving parent's heart would melt. They would be so grateful for this tenderness of spirit, this honesty, this openness. This is how God receives our confession. God's tenderness meets our brokenness. God's love and mercy enfold us and bless us. God's Spirit moves in us to heal us and set us free.

When we become aware of thoughts or actions that are destructive, self-serving or hurtful to others our instinct may be to react out of fear or shame. As a result we may deny or minimize our wrong doing and do everything we can to avoid God.

But what we need in these moments is to run to God. We are invited by God, welcomed by God, to run into God's loving arms and say with the psalmist, "God have mercy on me, heal me, I have sinned."

I need your mercy,
I need your help.
I have sinned against you
and others.
I need your healing.
I need your help.
I long to live a life of love.
But I fall short.
In your great mercy,
heal me.
Set me free.

Prayer suggestion:

Sit quietly, reflecting on God's mercy. As you are ready, confess your failings to God. Be specific about the ways you have fallen short. Ask God's Spirit to reveal anything else you need to confess. Ask God to heal you and free you to love as God loves.

Ask God to direct you to a spiritual friend or mentor and, with their permission, share your confession with them.

Having a Broken and Contrite Heart as Prayer

You do not delight in sacrifice, or I would bring it,
you do not take pleasure in burnt offerings.
The sacrifices of God are a broken spirit;
a broken and contrite heart,
O God, you will not despise.
Psalm 51:16-17

Prayer is being broken-hearted and contrite before God. The more we become aware of our shortcomings and character flaws, the more our hearts open in empathy and sorrow for those we have hurt. The more we see our pride, our greed, our self-serving and our defensiveness, the more we live in prayerful broken heartedness.

This text from Psalm 51 is part of a larger prayer of repentance by this psalmist. He has sinned. And he has been confronted with his sin. He sees how he has turned his back on God and gone his own way, causing pain and destruction to others. He sees all of this. He longs to make it right. He knows that an increase in religious activity is not what is needed. What is needed is a broken and contrite heart.

The dynamic at work here is not one of self deprecation or self punishment. It does not help us, or heal us, or change us when we beat ourselves up. A broken and contrite heart is not a heart full of self hatred. Self hatred and shame only keep us locked in our self focus. Self hatred and shame only lead to more of the same.

The dynamic at work when we are broken and contrite before God is the dynamic that is referred to in Scripture as "godly sorrow" (II Corinthians 7:10). According to this text, it is "godly sorrow that leads to repentance". Godly sorrow opens us to the transforming work that God's Spirit desires to do in our lives.

The focus in our brokenness is not, "What a terrible person I am." The focus is on the pain we have caused other people. What needs to break our hearts is the pain that our pride, our judgment, our disrespect, our deceit, our lack of compassion, our selfishness, our withholding of love, our greed, our addiction, our obsessions, our attempts to "fix," our inability to communicate our emotions, or our self righteousness have caused other people.

Living prayer is allowing our hearts to be broken in sorrow over the hurt we knowingly and unknowingly cause. Prayer is asking God to cause the hard shell of our defensiveness to break and fall away so that God's Spirit can enter our hearts and minds in a new way.

The good news is that God does not despise our broken, contrite hearts. God welcomes us in this state. God sees our prayerful brokenness as an act of worship. This is because we are receptive to God's healing grace when we are in this state. When we come to God with a broken and contrite heart, God's grace flows into this place of brokenness. This grace begins to free us and to flow through us and out to others. Our broken, contrite hearts become the fertile soil in which the love of God takes root.

Sometimes I hurt other people.

In attempts to protect myself,

I hide my vulnerability,

I horde my time,

I turn a deaf ear,

I harden my heart,

I hang on to resentments,

I obsess,

I judge others,

I imagine myself superior.

I see this. I see the pain I cause.

My heart is broken, God.

Have mercy on me.

Receive my broken and contrite heart.

Heal me. Set me free.

Prayer suggestion:

Sit quietly before God. Reflect on what you have been seeing during times of prayerful inventory and confession. Ask God to give you a broken and contrite heart about the ways you have hurt others. Ask God to fill you with empathy and compassion for people you have hurt. Offer your broken, contrite heart to God.

Repenting and Making Amends as Prayer

"The time has come," he said.
"The kingdom of God is near.
Repent and believe the good news!"
Mark 1:5

Zacchaeus stood up and said to the Lord, "Look, Lord!
Here and now I give half of my possessions to the poor, and
if I cheated anybody out of anything, I will pay back four
times the amount.
Luke 19:8

A life of prayer includes acts of repentance and making amends. To repent is to feel so much sorrow for the pain we have caused others that we commit ourselves to change for the better. To repent is to turn around. To go the other way. To change.

Honesty with ourselves and God, taking inventory, making confession and experiencing brokenness all lead to repentance. They all lead us to make different choices. They lead us to make amends for the wrongs we have done and the hurt we have caused. The goal is to exhibit real changes in our behavior, so that our destructive, hurtful choices are exchanged for life giving, healing choices.

But making changes in our behavior is not easy. It is not something that we can simple will ourselves to do. True repentance and change comes as we surrender our lives and wills to God's loving care and allow God to change us daily.

When Jesus calls us to repentance, he says two things. First he tells us that the kingdom of God is near. Then he calls us to believe this good news. Both of these things are directly related to acts of repentance and making amends.

What does it mean that the kingdom of God is near? How is this good news? And how does this bring repentance and change to our lives? Jesus is saying that God is with us. God is near. God, who is love, God who loves us, God who is our Maker and Healer, is with us.

Zacchaeus was a man who robbed from other people as he collected taxes for the Roman government. Not only did he collect taxes, but he collected enough extra to make himself a wealthy man. All this changed after Jesus spent some time at Zacchaeus' house. Zcchaeus' encounter with Jesus allowed Zacchaeus to experience personally the God who is with us and loves us. As a result, Zacchaeus repented and made amends, restoring what he had taken from others.

Remembering that we are loved, remembering who God is, remembering that God is with us, remembering that God calls us to live in love—this is the good news Jesus calls us to. The living, active truth of these realities is what gives us the power to repent, change our ways and make amends.

Repentance and making amends are prayer.

When I realize the ways in which
I have brought pain to others
through my selfishness, my pride,
my greed, my self protection,
my heart is broken in sorrow.
I repent. I turn around.
I seek, with your guidance,
to make amends to those I have hurt.
I know, God, that the kind of change I need to make
can only come by your healing power.
So I give myself again today to you.
Change me.
Give me the courage, humility and honesty I need
to make amends to those I have harmed.

Prayer suggestion:

As you sit in quiet, ask God to show you how you need to repent and change. Ask God to show you what amends you need to make to people you have wronged. Invite God to do this work in you and through you, as you surrender your life and will to God's loving care.

Keep in mind that the amends you need to make may include a conversation with the person you have harmed, inviting them to express the pain for which you are responsible. In this conversation your part is to acknowledge the pain you caused without asking for forgiveness and without offering excuses or pointing out their faults.

Keep in mind, as well, that making amends might also include the prayer of daily asking for God's help to live in love toward the person(s) you have harmed.

Ask God to guide you to a pastor, friend, sponsor or counselor who can offer you wisdom as you seek to change and to make amends.

Prayer as Healing

When we are honest with ourselves we know that we fail at the most important thing in life. We fail at love. God tells us: "I love you with unfailing love. My will for you is that you love like I love. Open your heart to me, attach yourself to me, love me and my love will begin to flow through you to others. Love your neighbor. Do to your neighbor what you want them to do for you—live in respect, honor, compassion, kindness and fairness to all."

Instead of seeing this as our true calling in life, we choose our own selfish, self-serving paths. We withhold love. We judge. We devalue. We hardened our hearts. We seek our own pleasure and comfort at other's expense. We continue in our addictions and attempts to control, harming many others in the process. We are full of greed and pride. In all these ways and more we fail at love. We hurt others. And we rob ourselves.

We wound and are wounded. And we are powerless to change ourselves. We are unable to heal what is broken inside us and between us.

We need God to heal us. We need God to free us to love.

The dynamic relationship with God that is prayer opens the way for this deep, life changing healing. Prayer is the experience of God's healing love in our lives.

Receiving Forgiveness as Prayer

If we confess our sins, he is faithful and just
and will forgive us our sins
and purify us from all unrighteousness.
I John 1:9

God is a forgiving God. God extends the gift of forgiveness to us, asking us to receive it as a gift. Not glibly, as if nothing has happened. Not proudly as if we have earned this gift. But with godly sorrow and humility we are asked to receive the gift of forgiveness that God offers.

God offers to restore our sense of innocence. God offers to restore our sense of being valued and loved. God offers to make us whole again.

It is life transforming to receive the gift of forgiveness. Unfortunately, receiving the gift of forgiveness is not always easy.

We may find ourselves afraid that we will "let ourselves off the hook." We may notice that we are hesitant to release our heavy load of guilt and shame. We may believe that we have to do something to "earn" God's forgiveness. We may feel that we deserve to be punished and—if God will not punish us—we may feel the need to do the job ourselves.

Some of our difficulties in receiving the gift of forgiveness are rooted in our beliefs about God. It is often difficult for us to take in the amazing grace and abundant forgiveness which flow continually from the heart of God. We may not see God as the fully, freely forgiving God that Scripture portrays.

In addition to our distortions about God, we sometimes have difficulty receiving God's forgiveness because we cannot forgive ourselves. Our expectations of ourselves may be that we should never fail. We may connect our sense of worth to our attempts to "get it right." As a result, when we do sin, when we do fail, we may be harsh and punitive toward ourselves.

In order to receive God's gift of forgiveness, we will need to release the shame we feel and embrace humility instead. Shame says to us, "You are a terrible person because of what you did." Humility says, "What you did was terrible, and you are, like all humans, a precious but flawed being who is loved by God."

In order to receive the gift of God's forgiveness, we need to be willing to let go of both the pride and the self-judgment that harden us against God's grace. We need to ask for an open, humble, child-like spirit.

In order to receive forgiveness we can ask for God's help to know that we are loved by a merciful, forgiving God. We can ask for the grace to embrace the truth that God wants us to receive the gift of forgiveness.

Prayer is opening our hearts and minds to receive God's gift of forgiveness.

You offer forgiveness.
Full, free, without reservations,
no small print with difficult to understand conditions.
Yet I do not find it easy to receive.
Sometimes I seem quite attached to
my feelings of guilt and shame.
If I receive forgiveness will I have to find a way
to live without these familiar companions?
Who will I be without my guilt and shame?
And I wonder if there isn't some catch.
Sometimes I have that too-good-to-be-true feeling.
I seem to have a hard time trusting
that you are really this generous in your forgiveness.
I have become accustomed to the expectation
of judgment and punishment.
Which is completely different from what you have offered.
Forgiveness.
So this is a big change for me.
I open my hands and heart,
help me to receive the life changing
gift of your forgiveness.

Prayer suggestion:

Talk to God about any difficulty you may experience in receiving forgiveness.

Ask God to open your heart and mind in the sorrow of repentance for all you need to confess. Make your confession to God. Ask God to show you what else you need to confess. Ask God to show you others to whom you need to make amends for ways you have been hurtful.

Ask for God's help to embrace the truth that God wants you to receive the gift of forgiveness like a little child might receive forgiveness from a loving, compassionate parent. Picture yourself as a child who knows they are loved, and who, once forgiven, feels both gratitude and a desire to practice kindness and goodness. Open your hands and heart to receive God's gift of forgiveness.

Forgiving as Prayer

When they came to the place called the Skull, there they crucified him, along with the criminals—one on his right, the other on his left. Jesus said, "Father, forgive them, for they do not know what they are doing."
Luke 23:33-34

Forgiving others is a form of prayer. It is not easy for us to receive forgiveness. And it is not easy for us to forgive. Our tendency is to want to hold on to our resentments. The wounds we have sustained feel deep and permanent, leaving us believing that we need to permanently hold on to our anger. Our anger and resentments often feel so righteous and justified that we can't see any wisdom in releasing them.

Yet, we hear Jesus, who has been falsely accused and wrongly put to death, praying, "Father, forgive them, for they know not what they do."

This is the prayer of forgiveness. It is a prayer of releasing those who have wronged us. When we are given the grace to pray this prayer with Jesus, we not only release those who have hurt us, but we, too, are released. We are released from our hardness of heart. We are released from bitterness and resentment. We are freed to love and to know ourselves loved.

In Richard Foster's book *Prayer*, he tells the story of a prayer found written on a piece of scrap paper in a Nazi concentration camp. The prayer is a prayer of forgiveness that shows us the open heartedness and healing grace that are the heart of forgiveness. The note read:

O Lord, remember not only the men and women of good will, but also those of ill will. But do not only remember the suffering they have inflicted on us, remember the fruits we bought, thanks to this suffering: our comradeship, our loyalty, our humility, the courage, the generosity, the greatness of heart which has grown out of all this. And when they come to judgment, let all the fruits that we have borne be their forgiveness. (Richard Foster, *Prayer: Finding the Heart's True Home*. HarperOne, 1992. pg 224)

Such generosity of spirit comes from the heart of God. The prayer of forgiveness is a prayer that comes to us as a gift. It is a gift that comes to us as we surrender ourselves and our resentments to God.

The prayer of forgiveness is a prayer of love. To receive forgiveness is to experience the power and tender kindness of love. To forgive is to allow the power and tender kindness of love to flow through us.

Frequently the prayer of forgiveness for those who have most deeply hurt us comes toward the end of a process of healing. When the fear, shame and guilt we have carried have been undone by God's grace, we are released. And in turn, we are ready in a deep way to release those who have hurt us. Only when we have experienced the truth that God's love is more powerful than any evil and any wound and we have experienced the healing power of God's love are we set free to let God's forgiving grace flow through us to others.

Teach me to forgive like you forgive.
Open my heart to the grace
and generosity of spirit
that Jesus had towards those
who falsely accused him
and crucified him.
Heal me so that I can know
myself to be your much loved child.
Show me that your love is more powerful
than any wrong, any hurt.
May your forgiving grace
flow into me and through me,

Prayer suggestion:

In a time of quiet ask God to show you who you need to forgive.

Honestly acknowledge your thoughts and feelings about extending forgiveness to this person.

Ask God to open your heart so that God's gift of grace and forgiveness can flow through you to this person.

Asking for Healing as Prayer

O LORD my God, I called to you for help
and you healed me. Psalm 30:2

The truth is that we are not well. We are full of fear and anxiety. We struggle with shame. We are caught up in obsessions and addictions. We are blind to our greed and pride. We are defensive, hard hearted and reactive. We are self centered. We fail to live as if we—and all others—are loved and valued beyond measure by our Maker.

Not only are we spiritually ill, we are unable to heal ourselves. We are powerless over our fears. Over our despair. Over our shame. Over our obsessions and addictions. Over our greed and pride. Over our reactivity. Over our defensiveness. Over our selfishness. We are powerless over our belief that we are worthless and unlovable. We are powerless over our blindness to other people's worth in God's eyes.

But God's love is powerful enough to heal all our brokenness. God's love is powerful enough to free us from our fear and shame and despair. God's love is powerful enough to free us from our obsessions and addictions, from our greed and pride, from our reactivity and defensiveness and selfishness. God's love is powerful enough to help us know ourselves and others as dearly loved and deeply valued.

It is only fair, however, to offer a warning about the process of experiencing God's healing in our lives. When we begin to encounter our spiritual illness and turn to God for healing, we often encounter an experience similar to going to a medical doctor. When someone goes to a doctor with what seems like a minor complaint and finds out that they have cancer, things go from bad to terrible. The problem turns out to be worse than

163

they thought. And the treatment designed to free them from a disease may create significant distress before it helps them feel better.

This is often the experience we have when we seek spiritual healing from God. God begins to shine a light on the problem so that we see it more clearly. This can be a disturbing and uncomfortable experience. God's healing may involve opening up our festering wounds to clean them out. During times like this things can feel like they are getting worse rather than better. We may be tempted to stop receiving this kind of help. We may decide we don't want this healing. We may be tempted to believe that we are beyond hope. But, as with most treatments for life threatening illnesses, the pain is part of the process of receiving the deep healing we need.

Prayer is inviting God to heal us and free us. It is in the process of showing up for our Healer's treatment, over and over and over again, that we can be set free and made whole.

I am powerless over my fears,
heal me, I pray.
I am powerless over my despair,
heal me, I pray.
I am powerless over my obsessions,
heal me I pray,
I am powerless over my self-centeredness,
heal me, I pray.
Oh Power far greater than myself,
Oh Healer of my soul,
come, heal me,
set me free.

Prayer suggestion:

Ask God to help you to make a list of the diseases of your mind and soul.

Bring each item on the list to God for healing. Invite God to heal you fully.

Entrust each area of brokenness to God's loving care.

Spend some time in quiet in the presence of God, your Healer.

Letting Go of Fear as Prayer

God is our refuge and strength,
an ever-present help in trouble.
Therefore we will not fear, though the earth give way
and the mountains fall into the heart of the sea,
though its waters roar and foam
and the mountains quake with their surging.
Psalm 46:1-3

Scripture often speaks to our fearful human hearts. "Do not be afraid, God is with you," is a common theme we find throughout Scripture. Even if the earth gives way and the mountains fall, we do not need to fear because God is with us as our refuge and strength. Even when we walk through the valley of the shadow of death, we do not need to be afraid, because God is with us as our comfort and guide. No matter what we encounter, no matter what makes our human hearts faint with fear, we are not alone, we are loved, God is with us.

Unfortunately, it is fairly common for fear to become the central feature of our lives. When this happens our fear can lead us to obsessions, addictions and frustrated attempts to control ourselves and others. Fear can lead us to judge and attack anyone who seems to be a threat. Our fears leave us agitated, depressed and full of dread.

It is true that there is much to be afraid of in this world. We fear all kinds of losses. We fear death. We fear humiliation and rejection. We fear pain. We fear loneliness. We fear meaninglessness. We fear the unknown. We fear fear itself.

But most deeply of all, we fear that we are on our own in this world. We fear that we are not loved or valued by our Creator. We fear that we are judged, condemned and abandoned by the

One who made us.

What we long for most is to know that we are loved and valued and that no matter what happens in life, we won't have to face it alone—we will be given the help, strength and grace we need. We long to know that we can find refuge in the loving arms of God.

Prayer often involves listening to the Spirit speak tender, powerful, personal reassurances to us when we are afraid. Prayer is listening deeply to the surprising and life giving words of God, "Don't be afraid, I am here with you. I am your refuge. I am your help and strength. I am here always. You can find comfort and rest in my loving arms."

God calls us out of the many traps that fear can create in our lives. God does not promise us a life free of suffering and loss. But God faithfully, persistently promises to be with us through all of life, bearing our sorrows, and giving us strength, comfort and hope even in the darkest hours.

Prayer is a response to God's call to release our fears to God and to know that God is powerfully, lovingly present with us in all of life.

You know my fears.

You know how they come unbidden to my heart and mind.

In the middle of the night. In the light of day.

You know my fear of loss and death and abandonment.

You know my fear of fear.

You know all the things I do in

an effort to keep these fears under control.

And you know the problems that are created

when I try to control the uncontrollable.

So I bring my fears to you.

Help me to listen deeply to your voice of love.

Remind me again that you are with me—no matter what.

Remind me that you are my refuge and my strength.

When all is well and when the mountains fall.

Be my safety, my hope, my refuge, my ever-present help.

Prayer suggestion.

Ask for God's help as you list the fears that commonly distress you. Next to each fear write down what you do in reaction to this fear (try to control others, withdraw from others, distract yourself, etc.) Talk with God about what you have written.

Ask for help to listen as God says to you, "I am your refuge and strength. I am with you now and always. Do not fear. You are not alone. I love you. I am with you to help you."

As you are ready, release each fear, and each attempt to deal with it on your own. Acknowledge to God the ways in which you hurt others because of your fears. Picture yourself resting in God's loving arms.

Making Room for Hope as Prayer

May the God of hope fill you
with all joy and peace
as you trust in him,
so that you may overflow
with hope by the power of the Holy Spirit.
Romans 15:13

Prayer is the act of making room within us for the gift of hope. Hope does not come naturally to us. For many of us, despair is what comes most naturally. We have a tendency to project our worst fears into the future. We imagine terrible things. Worst of all, we imagine terrible things while also imagining that we will be alone. Sometimes it seems like all of the space within us that God wants to fill with hope is already full of fear, despair and loneliness.

Hope is not the denial or avoidance of these painful realities. It is not a kind of pretending that everything is fine. Hope is, rather, the experience of looking into the future and seeing glimpses of God's goodness and grace. It is the capacity to trust that God's love is stronger than all the powers of hate, greed, or injustice in this world. Hope is the faith that whatever our circumstances, we are held in the loving heart of God.

Hope is a gift—a gift offered to us by the God of hope. Prayer brings us into direct contact with the God of hope. In prayer, we open ourselves to God's living reality, to God's healing and to God's redemptive activity in our lives and in the world. In prayer, we catch glimpses of what God's healing and blessing might look like in the future.

This prayer from the book of Romans is a prayer that we will come to trust the God of hope. It is as our trust in God deepens that we open ourselves to be filled with joy, peace and hope. As we give up reliance on ourselves, as we let go of trying to be in control, as we stop listening to the cacophony of voices of fear all around us, as we begin to trust, rest, rely on the God of hope, we make room for the gifts of hope that God offers us.

God will give us new eyes to see beyond our circumstances, beyond our fears, beyond our despair. God will give us new eyes to see the power of God's goodness and love at work in our lives and in this world. God will open our minds and hearts to trust that God holds us, and all that is, in God's loving, tender, powerful hands. In all of this God will heal our fears and fill us with peace. God will heal our sorrow and replace it with joy. God will fill us with an overflow of hope in the One who is our hope.

May we open our hearts in the prayer of making room for hope.

Free me
to let go of self-reliance,
to let go of fear and despair.
Teach me to trust you,
allow me to make room for your gift of hope.
May I trust
the power of your love
in my life and in this world.
Give me eyes to see anew.
Fill me to overflowing with
your peace,
your joy,
your hope.

Prayer suggestion:

In a time of quiet, picture your heart as a container.

Notice any fear or despair that are in this container.

Notice any self-reliance that fills this container.

Ask God's Spirit to heal your fear and despair and self-reliance.

Ask God to strengthen your trust in God's goodness and love for you.

Ask the God of hope to fill the container of your heart with gifts of hope.

Holding Fast as Prayer

*Be very careful to keep the commandment and the law
that Moses the servant of the LORD gave you: to love the
LORD your God, to walk in all his ways, to obey his commands, to hold fast to him and to serve him with all your
heart and all your soul.*
Joshua 22:5

Prayer is sometimes holding on to God. Holding fast is
something that infants do when they catch your finger in
their little hand and hang on tightly. The image of an infant
grasping the finger of a loving adult is a helpful way for us to
think of the prayer of holding fast. In the daily uncertainties
of life and in times of great difficulty, we can hold on to God.
When we see ourselves acting in ways that are self-serving, when
we are prideful or defensive,we can return to the humility and
surrender of being a small child, holding on to God.

When we are uncertain or afraid holding fast to God helps
us remember that we are not alone. When we are faced with
our powerlessness, our selfishness, our pride or our attempts to
control what we cannot control holding fast helps us remember
that there is a Power greater than ourselves. Holding fast helps
us remember who we are as God's loved child.

The image of an infant hanging on to a loving parent's finger
is greatly enriched by the fact that while the baby holds on, the
baby is being securely held. The one who holds on is being held.
Held securely. If the infant does not feel secure in the arms of
the adult, she would be grasping and clinging in desperate ways
Sometimes we may feel like a child who thinks she is about
to be dropped. We grasp and cling to God out of fear that we
will be abandoned or rejected. Our reaction may be shaped by

172

memories of feeling insecure as a child with inattentive adult caretakers. We forget that God is not like those wounded and distracted humans. We forget that we are secure in God's arms.

The context for this call to hold fast to God, is the context of love. We are able to 'hold' fast to God because God has always been holding us securely.

God whispers to us, "I love you. Let's live in loving relationship. I will show you how. I will hold you while you hold fast to me."

In order to wrap our child-like fingers around one of God's fingers, we will need to open our closed fists and let go of all the things to which we normally cling. We will need to let go of all that we grasp at in an attempt to feel secure. We will need instead to learn to hold fast to the one reality that is our true security—the Love of God which calls to our hearts and souls. This letting go in order to hold on to God is at the heart of our healing. Letting go so we can hold fast sets us free.

You invite me to hold on to you.
All the time you are
holding on to me.
Thank you for holding me,
and loving me through all of life.
Give me the daily grace to let go
of all the false securities to which I cling.
Give me the freedom that comes
from holding fast to your Love.

Prayer suggestion:

In a time of quiet, picture yourself as an infant, held securely in God's loving arms, holding fast to God.

Prayer as Expressing Distress

Life is full of gifts. We are continually being blessed with an outpouring of God's grace, kindness and love. But life is also full of suffering. To live as humans on this planet is to know suffering—physical suffering, emotional suffering, spiritual suffering. Sometimes this suffering is brought on by our destructive choices. Sometimes by our deep seated fears. Sometimes by the choices of others. And sometimes by forces unknown to us.

Humans tend to seek meaning in life events. We attempt to find meaning in our suffering. We look for causes. We may imagine that suffering is a sign of God's punishment or God's abandonment. We may fear that our suffering is the result of our failure to be perfect enough or good enough. We may blame others for problems they did not create.

All of this can add more distress to the distress we are already experiencing. Our fears about the meaning of our suffering can multiply our suffering.

God's voice calls to us in the midst of this distress and says: "Call on Me in times of trouble," God instructs us to take our distress, all of it, to God. God invites us to come with all our pain and fear and anguish.

When we share our suffering with a friend who is compassionate and trustworthy, we find comfort. And the intimacy of the relationship deepens. And so it is with God. When we express our distress to the God of Compassion, we will begin to experience a new depth to our intimacy with God. As we invite God to enter our suffering with us, we will find ourselves surprised by the ways in which God strengthens us, helps us and comforts us.

Lament as Prayer

My God, my God, why have you forsaken me?
Why are you so far from saving me,
so far from the words of my groaning?
O my God, I cry out by day, but you do not answer,
by night, and am not silent.
Psalm 22:1-2

This psalm gives expression to our deepest suffering. God absent. God silent. God hidden. God forsaking us. Even Jesus cried out to God from this place of terrible darkness. As he was dying Jesus echoed the words of the psalmist. Jesus lamented, "My God, my God, why have you forsaken me?". Margaret Bullitt-Jonas' observations about this prayer from the cross capture the reality of this kind of lament:

> Jesus experienced total abandonment on the cross, for although God the Father in fact was with him, God the Son knew nothing about it. In the wilderness of our own desolation we too, like Jesus, may have no felt awareness that God is near....As far as we know we are abandoned and alone. Yet even in the center of apparent abandonment, God is with us. God embraces the void. God doesn't take it away. God doesn't wipe it out. Instead, with an overflow of compassion, God shares the void with us. Like Jesus, we don't see God at all; all we know is the void. But the void is in God. (Margaret Bullitt-Jonas, *Our Passion, Christ's Passion.* Cowley Publications, 2003. pg. 56)

We may intellectually affirm that God is always with us. We may want to trust that this is true. But our experience is sometimes dramatically different from our intellectual affirmations. Instead of God's presence, we sometimes experience a terrible emptiness. It is as if the lights suddenly go out and we find ourselves alone.

Often the darkness of the experience of God's absence is made more painful by our self accusations. We feel in darkness like we are spiritual failures. We feel like something must be terribly wrong with us. Others may add to this pain by trying to fix what cannot be fixed. We may be told to pray harder or longer or more sincerely. Or to "just trust God". This kind of well intentioned advice may leave us feeling not only abandoned by God but also abandoned by our friends and helpers.

We do well to remember that Jesus knows what it is like to experience the anguish of this ultimate abandonment. And to remember that God did not abandoned Jesus. Nor does God abandon us. But Jesus experienced this pain with us and, in suffering it with us, he demonstrated his ability to carry our deepest sorrows.

When we experience a sense of God's absence we are in good company. The psalmists, the prophets, many people of faith, and Jesus himself knew this kind of spiritual suffering. We do not need to add to our suffering by seeing these dark times as evidence of failure. What we can do is join the psalmist and Jesus in giving voice to our spiritual distress. We can let our lament be our prayer.

Where are you?
Day after day,
night after night,
I suffer alone.
I need your help,
I need your comfort,
I need your guidance.
But you are silent.
Where are you, God?
Do not hide yourself from me any longer.
Why have you forsaken me?

Prayer suggestion:

Pray your own prayer of lament. Or let yourself enter the suffering of another (near or far away) who may be experiencing a need for God's presence. Pray a prayer of lament on their behalf.

Seeking God as Prayer

All night long on my bed
I looked for the one my heart loves;
I looked for him but did not find him.
I will get up now and go about the city,
through its streets and squares;
I will search for the one my heart loves...
Song of Songs 3:1,2

When we are suffering, when we need God the most, we may have the greatest sense of being abandoned by God. The suffering we experience may feel like evidence that we have been forgotten, or that we are not loved or valued by God. When we try to pray there may be no capacity to even hope that God's presence is with us. Our need for God in times of distress and our sense that God has disappeared adds suffering on top of suffering. "Where is God?" our hearts cry out.

The spiritual suffering that comes when God seems absent is compared in the Song of Songs to the desperate search of a woman for the one she loves. The woman in this poem has been waiting for her love. It is night and she is alone. She is so distraught that she gets up out of bed and runs wildly through the streets searching for the one her heart needs and loves.

Our wild seeking is also a form of suffering. But even this can become a gift to us. Our seeking can cause us to feel our need for God more directly, deeply, desperately. Our seeking can help us open our hearts more fully to receive the One our hearts longs for.

The reality is that the One we seek, never leaves us. Scripture tells us that God does not move away from us when we are crushed or broken hearted. Scripture tells us that God is close—

even in times of suffering.

Our suffering is known to God. Our suffering is shared by God. God's carries our sorrows. God bears our burdens.

What we need in times of distress is to lean into this possibility—this promise of who our Maker really is. It may feel like we have searched wildly through the city streets to find the One for whom our heart longs. It may feel like we need to muster up more strength and energy than we have in order to find the arms of Love that can comfort us. But we need not search any further than our next breath. We need not exert any more effort than it might take to form the word: "Help."

Our greatest longing in life is to know God's loving presence. Our greatest need in times of distress is to sense God with us. God is with us. In our joy and in our sorrow.

Our prayer of seeking God is our return to our heart's true desire. Our prayer is our remembering this One we love and turning again to find and be found.

Sometimes you seem to disappear.
Especially in times of distress.
It is as if I can't find you.
You are my heart's true home,
my deepest longing.
I seek you.
Let me find you.
I need you.
Let me know your presence.
Keep my heart and mind open
to your loving Presence with me.
May I seek you throughout the day today.
May I seek you and know your presence.

Prayer suggestion:

Recall a time when you felt as if you could not trust that God was with you.

Reflect on how this sense of being bereft of God's presence is part of your experience at the present time.

Put into words whatever desire you have to seek God and to know God's presence with you today. Listen as the Spirit whispers to your spirit, "I am here with you."

Grieving as Prayer

Be merciful to me, O Lord, for I am in distress,
my eyes grow weak with sorrow,
my soul and my body with grief.
My life is consumed with anguish
and my years with groaning;
my strength fails because of my affliction,
and my bones grow weak.
Psalm 31: 8-9

This text is a gripping and painful description of grief. It is a grief that goes on and on, a grief that consumes, a grief that wears one down physically and spiritually. We cannot live in this world without experiencing this kind of grief. To live is to suffer loss and the threat of loss. The question is, how do we live with loss? What do we do with our grief?

For too many people grief is something shameful, weak and unacceptable. It is, therefore, something denied and minimized. We talk about how we need to "get over it" and "move on." This may look brave and even strong. But it is not. The truth is that this kind of response to our losses is an attempt to avoid the pain of grief. It turns out that this way of navigating the pain of grief comes at a great price. It requires us to close and harden our hearts, rather than courageously opening our hearts to the reality of our grief and to the tender love and longing that are the heart of our loss.

We close our hearts to grief for many reasons. Perhaps the most important reason is not that we are trying to avoid suffering, but that we cannot bear such suffering alone. We need the love and comfort of others and of God in order to find the strength and courage needed to truly, honestly grieve.

We can find this kind of strength and comfort in God. Our prayers of grief are welcomed, even blessed, by God. Jesus began the Sermon of the Mount with this blessing: "Blessed are those who mourn, for they will be comforted." (Matthew 5:4) And Paul wrote from personal experience that God is the God of all comfort and the Father of all compassion to whom we can always turn. (II Corinthians 1: 3-4).

Sometimes prayer is the expression of grief. Our full, terrible, aching grief. Poured out to God as if God cares about our loss, our pain and our need for comfort. To grieve in this way is to be honest, humble, courageous. Most important of all, to grieve in this way is to open our hearts, rather than close them. To grieve in this way is to open our hearts in love. It is to express our love for what has been lost.

Grief is a terrible, yet beautiful thing. It is beautiful because to grieve is to let ourselves express our love with our whole body, heart and soul. When we pour our grief out in prayer we are pouring out our selves to God. We are promised that we will be met with God's healing love and comfort.

God, I am heavy with grief.

My mind is dark.

My body weighed down.

My heart is shredded.

It is hard to face the day.

Nothing seems to matter.

I need Your comfort.

I need You to hold me.

I need You to lift the crushing weight of this sorrow.

Have mercy on me.

Have mercy.

Prayer suggestion:

What losses have you suffered recently or in the past?

Write a prayer of grief about your loss. (The loss may be a person, a dream, an opportunity. It may be the loss of a parent's love you never had but always needed.)

Pour out your heart to God. Invite God to comfort you.

Pouring Out Our Hearts as Prayer

Trust in him at all times, O people,
pour out your hearts to him,
for God is our refuge.
Psalm 62:8

When we listen with an open heart to the outpouring of another person's heart, something happens. A bond forms. A closeness grows. And out of this relationship healing begins to take place.

But sharing one's heart requires trust in the other person. It requires trust that the other person will listen as accurately as possible, that the other person will genuinely care, that the other person will be respectful of our suffering. This trust grows over time as these qualities are experienced on a consistent basis.

God, the One whose name is Wonderful Counselor, invites our trust. God invites us to pour our hearts out. God offers to be our refuge—the place where we can find understanding, compassion and wisdom. For many of us, trusting God in this way may not be as easy as it might sound. We have all kinds of reasons to hesitate. We may feel confusion and shame about all that our hearts hold. We may not be able to imagine that our deepest feelings will be welcomed by God. We may not have experienced God as a Wonderful Counselor.

In order to respond to this invitation to pour out our hearts, we may need to start by taking small steps. We can begin by sharing some of what we are feeling with God. We can ask for the courage and hope to continue to trust more and share more with God. We do not do this to keep God informed. We do this to get the help we need from God. We do this so we can become whole.

As our trust in God's love, goodness and personal availability to us increases, our freedom to pour out our hearts to God will deepen. We will find ourselves freer and freer to share our sorrows, our joys, our questions, our fears, our longings, our doubt, our outrage and our resentments with the One who made us and loves us.

As we do this day after day, something happens to us and to our relationship with God. A bond forms. A closeness grows. And from this deepening relationship healing begins to take place in our hearts, minds and bodies. We experience comfort. We receive wisdom. We are corrected and restored. We are guided. And most of all, we are loved.

God is our true Counselor. God is the One who heals us and sets us free. May we respond to this invitation to trust God and to pour our hearts out to God. May we experience God more and more as our refuge and our safe place.

You ask me to trust you.
You invite me to pour my heart out.
I am amazed that you
love me this intimately.
I am amazed that you
ask me to share everything with you.
All the fear and joy and longing,
all the anger and confusion.
Everything.
Thank you for inviting me
to know you as my refuge.
Teach me to trust you more and more.
Teach me to pour my heart out to you
more and more,
so that our intimacy will deepen
and I will find wholeness.

Prayer suggestion:

Sit quietly. Breathe easily and deeply.

Ask God to free you to pour your heart out in prayer.

Talk to God about all that is on your mind and heart today.

Crying as Prayer

You are forgiving and good, O Lord,
abounding in love to all who call to you.
Hear my prayer, O Lord; listen to my cry for mercy.
In the day of my trouble I will call to you,
for you will answer me.
Psalm 86:5-7

Sometimes prayer is a cry from our heart. It is a raw pleading for mercy in times of trouble. There may be times of trouble when we find ourselves thinking, "I can't go to God in this time of trouble because I haven't been consistent in praying every day. How can I talk to God about my troubles when I haven't been talking to God on a daily basis?"

But God invites us to call for help in times of trouble no matter what. There are no pre-conditions we have to meet. There are no hoops we need to jump through. There is nothing we have to prove. We can simply cry to the Lord about our trouble and know that God will answer.

"God, you are forgiving. God, you are good. God you are abounding in love to all who call to you." This is how the psalmist begins his cry for mercy. It is as if the psalmist is reminding himself of the truths that he needs to hang on to during his time of trouble. We do well to do the same. We do well to remember who it is that we call to when we cry for mercy in times of trouble.

We cry out to a God who is forgiving. All that makes us want to hide in shame and guilt is seen and known by God and is met with an outpouring of compassion and forgiveness. We do not need to hide. We can come to God knowing that we will be received in love, knowing that God offers us forgiveness.

We cry out to God who is good. God the giver of life itself. God the giver every good and perfect gift. God who blesses and provides and heals and helps. This is the God who is powerful and eager to restore us in every way.

We cry out to God who is abounding in love for all who cry out for help and mercy. God loves us all. God is patient, kind, respectful, hopeful, faithful towards us all. God values us all. We are all seen and known and treasured by the One who made us. This One will hear our cry. This One will answer us.

Allowing ourselves to remember this good news can free us to cry to God. We do not need to hesitate for a moment when our hearts cry out. We can let that cry become our prayer. Whether our cry is for ourselves, for our loved ones, or for people we don't know but have only heard about, we can cry aloud to the Lord. Our cry will be heard by our loving and merciful God who will answer.

I am in great distress,
I cannot keep from crying aloud.
Receive my cries.
Have mercy.
Thank you that you are forgiving.
Thank you that you are good.
Thank you that you abound in love to all who call on you.
Thank you that you will answer.

Prayer suggestion:

What is happening in your life, in the life of someone you know or in the world that causes your heart to cry out at this time?

Let your heart cry become a prayer.

Cry aloud to the Lord.

Waiting as Prayer

I waited patiently for the Lord;
he turned to me and heard my cry.
Psalm 40:1

We live in a world of instant everything. We value speed. This is true not only in our culture at large, but in our spirituality. When we pray, we want to see results. And we want to see them now. Our need for quick results is especially urgent when we, or someone we love, is in distress. If we cry out to God in a time of distress and the distress continues or worsens, we are likely to question ourselves and to question God. We may wonder if we have done something wrong because our prayers are not being answered. We may wonder if God has abandoned us or if God cares about us.

Sometimes prayer is about waiting. Sometimes prayer is the practice of waiting patiently for God. To wait patiently for God is to trust in God's unfailing love for us. To wait patiently is to pray with hope that we are not abandoned or forgotten by God.

This is not an easy kind of prayer to practice. Most of us will need to pray for gifts of trust and hope as we wait for God. And even these gifts may be slow in coming.

If, however, we ask for the grace to practice the prayer of waiting we will find something changing in us. We will find that we are waiting not only for relief from our distressing situation but waiting for God's presence to be made known.

The prayer of waiting draws us into a place of stillness and quietness before God where we open our heart to listen and receive the good gifts of guidance, wisdom and blessing. Even more, the prayer of waiting is a prayer of following our heart's deepest cry, the cry for God to come to us, to be with us. Sometimes in such sacred but difficult moments of prayer God does remarkable things in us:

> Something happens to us in this kind of waiting. We are brought to attention. Our hearts and minds and spirits focus on what matters most, on what is most real, on our deepest longings for God....As we wait and watch in anticipation of the One-who-is-with-us to be revealed, a great work takes place within. A deeper container is carved in our souls—a container that will be able to receive more of God's life, more of God's love and grace. (Juanita Ryan, *Keep Breathing*. CreateSpace, 2009. pg. 102)

God is with us in our distress, in our sorrows, in our times of need. But sometimes we are invited to wait to see the evidence of God's loving activity in our lives. Sometimes we are invited into the prayer of waiting, so our truest longing can emerge and our hearts can be made ready to receive all that God has for us.

When we wait with hope it is like sitting in the dark of night before the first rays of dawn have appeared. We know the dawn will come, but we cannot hurry it. We can watch and wait with hope to receive the first lights with joy.

I wait.

I wait for you to answer.

I wait for the first light of dawn.

I wait for you.

I wait for you.

I wait for you.

I wait.

My waiting is my prayer.

In the pain of the waiting I feel my longing for you.

I long for you to be here.

I wait for your arrival, you who has always been here.

In the waiting I know a larger space in my soul is being excavated.

I can feel the growing emptiness.

But I know that it will be filled

with your gracious, loving presence.

Make me ready to receive you.

I wait.

Prayer suggestion:

What cry of your heart are you waiting for God to answer?

Picture yourself in an open space (a mountain meadow, the beach, the desert). It is a dark night. But you are awake, sitting in prayer, waiting patiently for the first rays of dawn, waiting for God to respond to the cry of your heart. Let your waiting be your prayer.

Prayer as Asking for God's Help

Why do we need to ask? Sometimes we struggle with this question in our human relationships. People close to us, we reason, should know what we need.

We tend to struggle with this question even more when it comes to our relationship with God. Certainly God knows what we need. Why do we need to ask God for anything? Shouldn't God provide what we need without our asking?

There is much, so much, that God provides without our asking. Every beat of our heart, every breath we draw are gifts. Every good and perfect gift, every one, is from God, our loving Father.

But still, we are told to ask. "Ask," Jesus said. Ask. It seems to be an important spiritual principle.

The gospels tell a story about two blind men who sat beside the road, begging. They heard that Jesus was walking by. They knew that Jesus had healed many people. So they called out to Jesus. Jesus stopped and talked with them.

"What do you want me to do for you?" Jesus asked them. Isn't it obvious? They are blind, they want to see. But Jesus engaged with them. He invited them to express their need, to give voice to their desire. "We want to see," they responded.

There are several gifts that come from our asking. First, we are given an opportunity to experience our need and desire more directly. Second, in our asking, we are given an opportunity to express our reliance on our Maker. And, third, when we ask, we are more likely to be on alert to watch for God's response and to take in the personalized care that we receive.

Prayer is not a matter of handing a wish list to God and expecting God to do our bidding. But this does not mean that prayer should be devoid of asking. Prayer is the gift of identifying our needs and longings and bringing them to God. It is the practice of living out the reality of who we are as God's much loved children, relying on God and asking for the help we need.

Bringing our Requests to God as Prayer

Do not be anxious about anything, but in everything, by
prayer and petition,
with thanksgiving, present your requests to God.
And the peace of God, which
transcends all understanding
will guard your hearts and your minds in Christ Jesus.
Philippians 4:6-7

God invites us to pray about every anxiety. Every time we are anxious we are invited "by prayer and petition, with thanksgiving, to present our requests to God." In spite of this clear invitation, however, we may feel hesitant to pray in this way. We may think that asking God for anything for ourselves is selfish. Or we may think of any admission of our experience of anxiety is less than spiritual.

But this text invites us to honesty and humility. Of course we are going to be anxious. Of course we have many requests we want to make. The good news is that God not only anticipates this but welcomes us and invites us to pray about all our fears and all our requests.

Anytime we find ourselves feeling anxious we can see our anxiety as a reminder to pray. We can run like little kids to God and tell God about our fears and our requests. As we do this we are reminded to express gratitude to God for who God is, for the ways God will guide us and help us, for the times we have experienced God's care and provision in the past. These acts of thanksgiving help us to focus on the reality of God's love for us. It helps us to entrust ourselves, once again, to God's care.

We are promised that when we do this we will be given an extraordinary gift. Our fear and anxiety will be replaced with peace. The peace of God, which is beyond our understanding, will guard our hearts and will guard our minds.

Whenever we are anxious we can go to God with our requests and receive more than we were able to ask or think. We receive the gift of an encounter with the Prince of Peace who loves us beyond telling.

Henri Nouwen wrote about the experience of prayer as making requests from a similar perspective:

> "Often prayer of petition is treated with a certain disdain... Prayer of petition is supposedly more egocentric because the person is putting his own interests first and trying to get something for himself...But the important thing about prayer is whether it is a prayer of hope...A man with hope does not get tangled up with concerns for how his wishes will be fulfilled. So, too, his prayer is not directed toward the gift, but toward the one who gives it. His prayer might still contain just as many desires, but ultimately it is not a question of having a wish come true but of expressing an unlimited faith in the giver of all good things." (Henri Nowuen, *With Open Hands*, Ave Maria Press, Notre Dame, Indiana 46556, pp 79, 82)

I am anxious.

I am afraid.

Thank you that I can come to you.

Thank you that you invite me to bring my requests.

Thank you for all the ways you have cared for me in the past.

Thank you that I can trust the outcome

of all of life's circumstances to you.

Prince of Peace, fill me with your peace.

I entrust myself and all my concerns

to your loving care.

Prayer suggestion:

What concerns or anxieties do you have?

Allow yourself to talk to God about your concerns, your anxieties and requests.

Take some time to thank God for who God is, for how God will care for you in this situation, for specific ways you have experienced God's care for you in the past.

Open your mind and heart to receive the gift of God's peace.

Practicing Examen as Prayer

In your anger do not sin;
when you are on your beds,
search your hearts and be silent.
Psalm 4:4

Examen is the practice of prayerful reflection at the end of the day. It is the practice of lying on our beds and silently searching our hearts. Examen is a practice that can help us identify where we are receiving God's help and where we are needing to ask for God's help.

Days tend to blur into each other. Moments of grace and grief are often not given the time of reflection they need. Examen is a form of prayer that involves stopping for a few moments before we end a day to pick up the shells that washed ashore during the day so that we can pay attention to them and receive the treasures they hold.

The purpose of the prayer of examen is to help us to grow in both self awareness and in awareness of God's presence with us each day. This prayer helps us to look for God with us in the joys and the struggles of every day life.

St. Ignatius wrote about the prayer of examen in *The Spiritual Exercises*. He saw the examen as a prayer that could be used by God to reveal the direction our lives were meant to take, even as it reveals on a daily basis the presence of God in the ordinary realities of life. Others have offered a simple structure for this kind of prayer. In *Sleeping With Bread: Holding What Gives You Life*, Dennis Linn, Sheila Linn and Matthew Linn suggest that we ask and answer the questions: "For what moment today am I most grateful?" and "For what moment today am I least grateful?" They offer many versions of these two questions. One might ask, "When did I feel most alive today?" and "When did I most feel life draining out of me?" Or, "What was today's high point?" and "What was today's low point?" (Linns, *Sleeping With Bread: Holding What Gives You Life*. Paulist Press, 1994. pgs 6-7).

When practiced on a daily basis, examining the things we are most grateful for each day can open our eyes and hearts to the many gifts God gives us each day. And the practice of examining the things that we experience as the most distressing each day can give us new wisdom and insight about things we need to let go of or change.

The practice of examen is something that parents can do with their children as they tuck them into bed. In making time for this kind of mutual sharing, the parent can offer the child support and affirmation for life's daily challenges and blessings. It is also something that spouses or friends can do together, on a daily or weekly basis. This way of using the prayer of examen can build deeper intimacy, allowing us to share our grief and our joy with each other.

The psalmist instructs us, "when you are on your beds be still and search your hearts." In practicing the prayer of examen, our hearts are opened in new ways to God's presence, help and guidance.

At the end of this day quiet me.
Help me to be still.
Bring to my mind and heart
the moments when I felt
most grateful or connected to life
and the moments when I felt
most distressed or drained of life.
Remind me of what touched my heart
and what distressed me.
Help me as I reflect on these moments.
Show me whatever you wish to show me,
about me and about you.
Thank you.

Prayer suggestion:

Choose the questions that you want to ask at the end of the day. "For what moment today am I most grateful? and For what moment today am I least grateful?" Or, "When did I feel most alive today? and When did I most feel life draining out of me today?" Or, "What was today's high point?" and "What was today's low point?"

You may want to light a candle or ask for God to guide you as you reflect in this way about your day. You may want to keep a journal of your nightly examen, or share your reflections with someone close to you.

Interceding as Prayer

My intercessor is my friend
as my eyes pour out tears to God;
on behalf of a man he pleads with God
as one pleads for a friend.
Job 16:20-21

In Richard Foster's book *Prayer*, he introduces the topic of intercession by saying, "Intercession is a way of loving others." In praying for someone else's well being we join our spirits with their spirits, our hearts with their hearts. We are in solidarity with them, sharing their suffering, their longings, their needs. We are expressing the truth of their value and worth. We are desiring their well being. We are loving them.

In this text Job is telling his friends. "I want God to see my tears. I need you, my friends, to also see my tears and to go to God on my behalf."

The prayer of intercession requires something from us. It requires our heart. When we hear and see the news, and our hearts want to turn away from the pain and suffering we see, the prayer of intercession calls us to stay present to the pain and to pray for those who are suffering. The same is true when we hear and see the pain of those near us. Our heart may want to minimize or turn away, but the prayer of intercession calls us to open our hearts, to share in this suffering, and to pray for God's help, strength and comfort.

We may wonder why we should bother to pray in this way. God already knows, yet God does not seem to be stopping the suffering. What good does it do to pray for others?

Some people talk about intercession as if the work of intercession was the work of begging an angry, distant, demanding God to somehow behave better than this and to show some mercy and kindness. Intercession then becomes a desperate attempt to convince God to do something God does not really want to do. It is no wonder that when this is our view we find ourselves quickly giving up on this kind of prayer.

But this is not the prayer of intercession. Intercession is God's invitation to join in active love for all of creation. God is a loving, merciful, powerful, generous, tender God whose work in this world is to heal and free and bless. In intercession we join the flow of healing grace and participate in God's loving work in this world.

When we pray, we pay attention to God's desire to heal and free and bless. We do not need to convince God to do this. God is already at work in the world in this way. And, amazingly, God invites us to join in this work through intercessory prayer. Doing so opens our hearts to others. It joins us to others near and far, to their suffering, to their needs, to their value, and to God's unfailing love for them.

Bring to my attention
those for whom you would have me intercede.
Give me the courage
to open my heart and mind
to their suffering and need.
Help me to sit with you in spirit,
as you sit with them,
pouring out love and compassion,
bearing their burdens
carrying their sorrows.
May I participate in the flow of your healing.
and blessing in their lives
as I pray for each one.

Prayer suggestion:

Sit quietly, breathing slowly and easily. Ask God to open your heart and mind in love and to bring to your awareness anyone for whom God would have you intercede. Allow yourself to "sit with" this person, to get a sense of what they might be feeling and needing. Allow yourself to be aware of God's active, tender love for this person. Join God's love and valuing of this person by praying for their healing, strengthening and blessing.

Persisting as Prayer

Then Jesus told his disciples a parable to show them that
they should always pray and not give up.
Luke 18: 1

Prayer is a way of life. Prayer is faithfulness. Prayer is persistence. Prayer engages us in conscious contact with God. In doing so, it offers to draw us into a life time relationship with our Source, our Life. Prayer is faithfulness to this relationship. Prayer also draws us into God's ongoing activity in this world —God's work of saving, healing, releasing, blessing. Prayer is persistence in inviting the power of God's healing love into our lives and into our world.

We are called to pray for ourselves, for our loved ones, for strangers and for our enemies. We are called upon to ask God to heal and save and bless. We are called upon to pray for peace and justice. And we are called on to keep on praying. To not give up.

There is a danger that we will grow weary or discouraged. We may not see the results we had hoped for in our lives or in the lives of those for whom we pray. As a result, we may want to give up hope and give up praying.

We are a culture that has come to expect the quick fix, the fast cure, the instant everything. We eat fast food and relate through instant messaging. And spiritually we think of miracles as God's instant cures. The value of persistence is not deeply breed into our vision or our instincts.

Our discouragement in praying comes not only from our hurry-up mentality. It can also come out of our fears. We may fear that God is not really powerful or that God does not hear us. Or that God is not loving. Or that God has abandoned us or those for whom we pray. Or that we have to perform in some special way to have our prayers answered. We grow fearful of these things as we pray and our fear tempts us to give up.

But the work of healing, reconciling, releasing and blessing that God is doing in our lives and in this world is a difficult work. It requires time. God is a faithful and gentle healer. We resist God's love. We resist God's healing. We resist but God persists, faithfully loving us.

God asks us to be persistent in our prayers for ourselves and others and to trust that God is faithfully at work to offer the healing and blessing for which we pray. In asking us to be faithful, God is asking us to be like God. God is asking us to persist in prayer, even as God persists in actively loving and healing.

Pray and keep praying. Ask and keep asking. Invite God to give you glimpses of the freedom and joy that you seek for yourselves and others. Hold those images, those glimpses, in your heart and mind and keep praying. God is a healing God. God is at work. God is powerful in love and compassion. Come back to this vision. Stay with this calling. In time you will see the green seedling pushing up through the ground and you will know that all those days and years that nothing seemed to be happening, a miracle was taking place.

.

I get discouraged
and distracted.
You call me to pray
and to not give up.
You ask me to be
faithful and persistent in prayer.
Give me gifts of hope
and glimpses of your heart's desire
so that I can pray
and keep on praying
for healing,
for release and for blessing
in my life and in the lives
of others.
Make me faithful,
even as you are faithful.

Prayer suggestion:

What or who have you given up praying for?

Ask God to guide you in praying again about this.

Ask God to help you to keep praying for healing and blessing.

Engaging in Battle as Prayer

Finally, be strong in the Lord and in his mighty power...
For our struggle is not against flesh and blood,...but
against the powers of this dark world and against the
spiritual forces of evil in the heavenly realms...Put on the
full armor of God so that...you may stand your ground.
Ephesians 6: 10-13

Prayer is standing strong in the middle of a spiritual battle. It is remembering that there is an unseen spiritual realm of darkness at work in this world, and an unseen spiritual realm of light and love that is also at work. Prayer is staying grounded in God's powerful love and light.

The point of praying with awareness that spiritual forces of darkness are at work is not to live in fear or despair. Quite the opposite. The point of praying in this way is to keep us mindful that God's love and light are far more powerful than all the darkness we may encounter in this life. No matter how great the forces of evil are in this world, the power of God's everlasting love is far greater.

We are told to rely on God's great power, to stand in the truth and strength of the power of God's active love. It is worth noting that the armor of God in this text is defensive armor. We are not to attack. We are to stand, knowing that we are safe in God's care.

The psalmists often sing of the power of God's love. In Psalm 89:2,8 we read:

I will declare that your love stands firm forever,
that you established your faithfulness in heaven itself.
O Lord God Almighty, who is like you?

211

You are mighty, O Lord,
and your faithfulness surrounds you.

The psalmist declares that God's "love stands firm forever." It
is in this faithful love that we can stand, no matter how great
the darkness may seem. God's love stands firm and powerful and
we can stand secure in the power of that love.

Most of us have had our own personal encounters with darkness. Sometimes the darkness can feel overwhelming. We may
be tempted to despair. We may be tempted to believe that the
power of darkness is greater than the power of God's light and
love. But the power of God's love is always at work and is always
more powerful than all the evil and all the darkness in this
world. Even in the hour of Jesus' arrest, torture and death—the
hour that Jesus called the hour "when darkness reigns" (Luke
22:53)—God's powerful love was at work, saving, redeeming,
healing, blessing us all.

In the middle of spiritual battle we may be tempted to fear
that we are not loved, that we are beyond hope, that God is not
truly loving or truly powerful. Prayer is remembering that these
are lies. Prayer is standing securely in the mighty power of God's
faithful love.

Sometimes the darkness
is all I see, all I know.
I become overwhelmed
and I am tempted to despair
and to run away.
But you call me
to stand
securely
in the mighty power of your love.
Strengthen me to stand
even in the heat of battle,
knowing your love is always
more powerful than any darkness.

Prayer suggestion:

Take a few moments to sit quietly, breathing deeply and easily. Picture the light of God's powerful love above your head. Let it descend on you like a gentle blessing, falling over you like a protective shield, moving under your feet like a strong foundation on which to stand. Let it fill your heart and mind, guarding your heart and mind with peace, filling you with joy. See yourself standing securely in God's powerful, faithful, unshakable love for you and for all that God has made. As you stand in this way, see yourself putting on a belt of the truth of God's powerful enduring active love, a breastplate of God's goodness, a helmet of God's saving grace and power, a shield of faith and shoes of peace. In your hand take the sword of the Spirit which is God's declaration of love and power. Stand securely in God's mighty love. Let your standing be your prayer.

Remembering as Prayer

On my bed I remember you;
I think of you through the watches of the night.
Because you are my help
I sing in the shadow of your wings.
Psalm 63:6-7

Sometimes prayer is remembering the ways in which God has helped us. It is common for us to carry in our minds and bodies the memories of events that have been difficult, frightening or traumatic. It is common for us to live out of the assumption that these difficult, frightening or traumatic events will repeat themselves in one way or another in our future. When we do this we literally scare ourselves. We live with anxieties about all the terrible 'what ifs'.

But when we practice the prayer of remembering the many ways that God has helped us, our vision of the future begins to change.

Mister Rogers once told the story of how his mother would always encourage him as a young boy to "look for all the helpers" whenever anything distressing happened. It is good advice. We sometimes get so focused on the distressing events of life that we don't notice all the helpers that God sends our way, or the ways that God's grace and presence sustain us or guide us through the dark and difficult times.

Remembering God's help in the past eases our fears about the future. This does not mean that we pretend about our fears or that we have any guarantees that our life will always be easy. In fact, we are all pretty much guaranteed that there will be challenges and difficulties throughout the various stages of life. But when we remember the specific ways that God has helped us in the past, we are able to trust more fully that God will continue to help us each day.

The psalmist uses the image of singing in the shadow of God's wing. It is the image of a baby bird, safe in the nest with its mother. Protected, nurtured, loved. We live and rest in the shadow of God's wing. Whatever comes, we are not alone. God is our help today and tomorrow, just as God has been our help in the past.

Remembering God's help can turn our fears and anxieties into hope. Remembering God's help is enough to make our hearts sing.

Sometimes in the dark of night
I lie awake
full of anxiety.

But sometimes, I stop myself
and I turn my mind to you
and reflect on the ways
you have helped me in the past,
all the ways you have been my
strength and comfort and guide.
When I remember your help
in the good times and the hard times,
my fears ease,
and my hope rises.
You, God, are my Help.
I rest in the shadow of your protective wings.
I sing songs of hope
because of your love and care.

Prayer suggestion:

Spend some time remembering specific ways that God has helped you in the past. Express to God whatever thoughts and feelings come to you as you reflect on God's help and care. Spend some time allowing yourself to rest safely and to sing— like a contented baby bird sheltered under God's wings.

Prayer as Hearing and Seeing

It is often suggested that prayer is talking to God. We talk, God listens. We tend to assume that if we haven't actually formed thoughts and words and expressed them to God, then whatever is going on isn't prayer. But, if prayer is about a dynamic relationship that is initiated and sustained by God, then it will involve much more than just thoughts that have been formed into words. In any intimate relationship we communicate by talking, but we also communicate in many other ways as well—most importantly by listening. So prayer includes more than just talking. It requires us to listen in a way that makes it possible for us to both hear differently and see differently.

Hearing and seeing require a set of activities that look much different than the activities commonly associated with prayer.

First, hearing and seeing what God has to show us requires that we stop talking. It requires us to be silent. It requires that we make room for the Other to speak.

Second, hearing and seeing requires that we put aside our own agenda. It requires that we step away from our ideas and opinions and ways of seeing things to see things through the eyes of the Other.

Third, hearing and seeing requires that we tune in and pay attention. It requires that we open our hearts and minds to really hear and understand what is being communicated.

And fourth, hearing and seeing what God has to show us requires a response from us. A response of surrender to whatever wisdom, direction, correction, grace or love is offered.

Listening as Prayer

The word is very near you; it is in your mouth and in your heart so you may obey it. Love the Lord your God, listen to his voice, and hold fast to him.
Deuteronomy 30: 14, 19

Many of us have only known prayer to be a one way conversation. We talk and God listens. But prayer is meant to be a two way conversation. Sometimes we talk. And sometimes we listen.

It is true that the biblical text urges us to pour out our hearts to God. It is true that we are invited to bring all our fears and concerns, all our needs, and all our mixed up feelings to God in prayer.

But we are also invited to listen to God. We are invited to listen for the courage and comfort we need. We are invited to listen for the wisdom and guidance we need. We are invited to listen for the correction we need. We are invited to listen to the Voice of unfailing love.

What an astonishing thing it is that God speaks to us. That God enters into direct, intimate conversation with us.

To hear God well we need to do a few things. First, we need to acknowledge whatever fears we have about hearing what God might say. We might be so convinced that God will shame us or threaten us or ask us to do what we don't want to do, that we may be afraid to listen. It is helpful to acknowledge these fears to God and to a close friend. It is helpful to begin to pray for the healing of these fears.

It is not necessary, however, to wait until our fears are resolved before we invite God to speak to us. God longs for us to listen to guidance, comfort, correction and love. But God often waits for us to turn, to choose, to invite. Our invitation creates an opening in our hearts and minds to receive whatever it is God has to say.

Having invited God to speak, we can begin to actively listen for God's voice. Unfortunately, many of us have difficulty listening to other people. And whatever makes it difficult for us to listen to others is likely to also get in the way of our efforts to listen to God. What we will need to do is to gradually put aside our own agendas and enter the world of the Other. This requires us to make space for the Other to speak, quieting our hearts and minds and bodies.

As we sense that we are hearing God's "still, small voice" we need to do what we can to listen well. When we listen to a friend, we sometimes misunderstand or misinterpret what we have heard. So we check to be clear. And so it is as we listen to the Spirit. We might ask God for confirmation of what we are hearing. And, we might seek the counsel of a trusted spiritual friend.

But listening to God does not require that we go through difficult religious rituals. This text from Deuteronomy reminds us that "the word is very near" us, "it is in our mouth and in our heart." God's voice of unfailing love and wisdom is in our heart. May we learn to listen well.

Thank you that you love me.

Teach my heart to trust your love.

Free my heart to respond to your love
with love.

And as I learn to rest in the intimacy
of your love for me

and my growing love for you,

may I learn to listen to your voice.

May I hear whatever you have
to say to me today.

Give me the grace to make space for you to speak.

Give me the grace to receive your words,

your guidance, your wisdom, your correction, your blessing.

May I listen well to your voice today.

Prayer suggestion:

Take some time to acknowledge whatever fears you have about listening to God. Talk to God about these fears, asking God to teach you that God's voice is the voice of unfailing love. Then, as you are ready, invite God to speak to you about whatever God might want to say to you today. Ask for ears to hear and a heart to receive God's voice of love. Then sit quietly for ten minutes or more, gently bringing your wandering mind back to God's loving presence. Continue to listen throughout the day. Write about anything you sense God might be saying to you. Share what you sense with a trusted spiritual friend.

Seeing as Prayer

I pray also that the eyes of your heart may be enlight-
ened in order that you may know the hope to which he
has called you, the riches of his glorious inheritance in
the saints, and his incomparably great power for us who
believe.
Ephesians 1:18,19

Prayer is seeing. Prayer is having our eyes opened. It is having
the eyes of our hearts enlightened to the hope to which
God calls us, to the riches available to us, to the incomparable
power of God.

We have been blind with fear. Fear that we were beyond the
reach of love. Fear that we were beyond hope. Fear that God
would never embrace us or love us as we are.

We have also been blinded by fear of the darkness in our
own lives and in the world around us. Fear that the darkness is
greater than the light. Fear that the light of God's unfailing love
is not powerful of enough to save us from ourselves or from the
darkness in this world.

And we have been blinded by our self preoccupation and
pride. We have been blinded by our self-reliance, our greed, our
defensiveness. Because of all our fears, we have lived in a fortress of our own making. We have tried to protect ourselves no
matter the cost to ourselves or others.

But prayer lets in the light of God's unfailing love. Brick by
brick our fortress walls begin to be removed as we continue in
a life of prayer. As the bricks come down, God's light comes
streaming in. Once we were blind, now we begin to see.

As God's light pours in and our eyes begin to open, we begin
to see the hope we have. God has been calling us. God has been

drawing us. God has been lovingly knocking at the door of our hearts. God has been calling us to know the hope of life with God now and always.

We also begin to see the richness God has for us. The richness of God's forgiving, healing love. The richness of having a relationship with our Maker. The richness of the peace and joy that grow in us as we take in the love of God more and more.

And we begin to see the incomparable power of God. The text goes on to say that this is the same power that raised Jesus from the dead and seated him at the right hand of God. We begin to see that the power of God's love is far greater than the power of the darkness in us and in the world around us. God, who raised Jesus from the dead, raises us.

God frees us more and more from our self-serving, from our pride, from our self-reliance, from our greed, from our fear, from our defensiveness. God frees us and raises us to live empowered by love.

Prayer is seeing. It opens the eyes of our hearts to the light of God's unfailing love. To the hope we have in this love, to the riches we have in this love, to the incomparable power of this love.

Open my eyes.
Help me to see
the hope to which you have called us,
the riches you have for us
the incomparable power
of your love.
I am blinded by fears.
Heal my fears.
Free me to see you
and to know
the hope,
the riches,
and the power
of your love.

Prayer suggestion:

Sit quietly, breathing easily and deeply.

Pray the prayer of this text for yourself, in your own words if you choose.

Pray it as well for others in your life.

Invite the Spirit to show you whatever God wants you to see today.

Hearing as Prayer

After the earthquake came a fire,
but the Lord was not in the fire.
And after the fire came a gentle whisper.
When Elijah heard it, he pulled his cloak over his face
and went out and stood at the mouth of the cave.
Then a voice said to him,
What are you doing here, Elijah?
I King 19:12-13

The context of this story from the first book of Kings is that the prophet Elijah has fled for his life from a real and present threat and has spent the night in a cave. While in the cave, he hears God asking him to go and stand on a mountain, because the presence of the Lord is going to pass by. After this instruction is given, a great wind comes, then an earthquake, then a fire. But none of these dramatic events were the voice of God. Instead, the voice of God came to Elijah in a gentle whisper.

We look for God, listen for God, try to hear God, but often we do so with misguided assumptions. We expect God to speak to us with great drama.

But, more often than not, God comes to us in a gentle whisper. The God of the Universe, the Creator and Sustainer of all things, comes to us intimately, gently, quietly. This says a great deal about God, about the intimacy of the conversation that God offers us. It also says something about us. It tells us that in order to hear God, we will need to still and quiet ourselves and listen for God's gentle whisper.

Imagine a kindergarten teacher on the first day of school with her new class. Picture the children sitting on a rug while the seasoned teacher sits on a child-sized chair, welcomes the chil-

226

dren and talks to them about the guidelines for the classroom. For the first few minutes of talking to the children, the teacher whispers. The children and their parents sit very still, very quiet and lean in to hear every word she has to say.

Prayer is allowing ourselves to be those little children, sitting at the feet of our Maker, hearing the gentle whisper of God, speaking words of welcome and of instruction.

The fact that God speaks in a gentle whisper does not mean that we will always like what we hear. In this story, God knows that Elijah is afraid for his life and is in hiding. But this frightened hiding is not what God wants for Elijah. So God confronts Elijah asking, "What are you doing here, Elijah?' Elijah explains his fear and his behavior and God listens. This is, in fact, the second time they have had this conversation. God's response is to call Elijah out of hiding.

In gentle, tender love God calls us out of our fear, out of our hiding. May we quiet ourselves to hear. May our spirits be moved by the quiet, powerful, intimate voice of God.

When I am afraid, I go into hiding.
I crawl into a cave
in an attempt to protect myself.
I need to hear your voice.
Quiet me.
Still my fearful heart.
Let me be a little child before you,
listening for your gentle whisper
of loving instruction.
Give me the courage
and strength I need
to hear your voice
calling me out of hiding
and into your loving will.

Prayer suggestion:

Take some time to still and quiet yourself. Perhaps it would help to first pour out your fears and concerns to God. Then sit in a comfortable position, breathing easily, with hands open on your lap, inviting God to say whatever God might choose to say to you at this time. Listen for the gentle, loving whisper of God. If what you hear is harsh or judgmental, gently redirect your attention back to the loving heart of God. You may need to do this several times. If what you hear is silence, know that God is there with you in the silence. If what you hear is wisdom or instruction, write down what you hear and ask for the strength to respond.

Listening to Scripture as Prayer

Let the word of Christ dwell in you richly.
Colossians 3:16

One way to pray by listening is to listen to Scripture using a simple approach known as *lectio divina*, which simply means divine reading. It is a way of reading Scripture that allows the Spirit to use the words of the text to speak directly and deeply into our hearts and lives. In this way of reading, we slow down our reading and we bring ourselves to the text. We invite the Spirit to use the words we read to speak to us in whatever way the Spirit might choose.

There are many different ways to practice *lectio divina*. All of them involve inviting the Spirit to open our hearts and minds to whatever we need to receive and hear. This is typically followed by reading a short portion of Scripture and then sitting quietly for three or more minutes with an openness to what has just been read. This reading and then sitting quietly to experience the text is usually repeated four times.

One approach to these four readings of the same short text involves reading the text, then sitting quietly, noticing what might stand out from the text. This is followed by a second reading and a time of quiet reflection on the text. The third reading is followed by a time of responding to the text by talking to God about it. And, finally, the fourth reading is followed by a time of simply resting in God's presence.

Another approach involves reading a short text four times with pauses of three or four minutes between readings during which one simply rests and allows the Spirit to speak through the words of the text during each of the times of quiet.

Another approach involves the reading of a short narrative

text several times, often from the gospels, and each time putting oneself in the story as a different character in the story. This often allows the story to come to life and provides an opportunity to experience various points of view in the story.

Combining Scripture reading with meditative prayer in this way can open us up to the voice of the Spirit in new ways. Lectio divina is a way of allowing the Spirit to use the words of Scripture to speak to us directly in ways that challenge, heal and bless us. It is a way of reading Scripture that allows for a direct encounter with the text and with the Spirit.

As we practice the prayer of listening to Scripture, the word of Christ comes to dwell in our hearts more richly. In the inner sanctuary of our hearts, we take in the words of Scripture like bread for our souls. We are fed by God's Spirit with spiritual food. We are nourished, so that our spirits grow stronger in the reality of the love and grace of God.

Give me ears to hear
and a heart to receive
whatever you desire
to show me today.
Open my heart
to the words of Scripture.
May your word
come to dwell
in me
richly.

Prayer suggestion

Ask God's Spirit to open your heart to receive the word God has for you today. Read a short portion of Scripture. Sit quietly with it for three minutes. Gently notice what comes to your mind and heart. Read it again, and again sit in silence with it for three minutes, reflecting on it. Read it again and let yourself respond by talking to God about it as you feel moved. Read it one more time, followed by sitting in silence for three minutes. This time simply rest in God's loving presence as you take in whatever has moved you as you have reflected on the text.

Being Counseled by God as Prayer

I will praise the LORD, who counsels me;
even at night my heart instructs me.
Psalm 16:7

One of the names for God in Scripture is "Wonderful Counselor." A counselor is someone who listens with respect and compassion to our questions and concerns. A counselor draws us out, helping us clarify what we are experiencing, where we need course correction and what we can do in order to change, heal and grow. Then, on the basis of this close, accurate and loving listening, a good counselor offers us advice and guidance.

God, our Maker, lives in close intimacy with us. We are deeply known and deeply loved. God cares about the burdens we carry, the uncertainties we face, the needs we don't know how to meet. Throughout the day, and even at night, God invites us to seek the Spirit's counsel about all that concerns us.

There probably have been many times when we have forgotten God's offer to counsel us. We struggle with difficult decisions, or labor under seemingly impossible circumstances, or try to figure out how to meet a need on our own. And all the time, God reminds us to seek the Spirit's counsel.

When we move from relying on ourselves to relying on God's counsel, our minds are likely to stop spinning and fretting. When we step out of the spin and pray, "Lord, show me what to do." our minds have an opportunity to quiet. We are free, then, to wait and listen for God's guidance.

In this quieter space there is an opportunity both for our fears to surface and for our hearts' desires to become clear. We may find ourselves talking with God about our feelings and longings. It is as if God, the Wonderful Counselor, helps us pour our hearts out in prayer. Now, not only are our minds quieted, but our hearts are open to receive the counsel we need.

The psalmist says, "I will praise the Lord, who counsels me, even at night my heart instructs me." As our minds quiet and our hearts open to God's counsel, the Spirit speaks intimately and tenderly to our hearts. We know that we are known. We know that we are loved personally. We know we are God's beloved children.

It is this loving, intimate relationship that heals us. It is the love of our Counselor that fills us with hope and gives us the courage and strength we need.

Our Wonderful Counselor does not throw out advice from a distance. Our Wonderful Counselor holds us in loving arms, listens carefully to the cries of our heart, quiets our spinning minds, comforts us with understanding and whispers the counsel we need directly to our hearts.

You are the Wonderful Counselor.
You know me intimately.
You offer to quiet my spinning mind,
to listen to my fears and my longings.
You offer to hold me in your love
and to whisper your counsel
to my heart.
Come, God,
counsel me.

Prayer suggestion:

What concerns do you need counsel about today?

Invite God to be your Wonderful Counselor.

Listen for the Spirit's whispers to your heart.

Being Taught by God as Prayer

Show me your ways, O LORD,
teach me your paths;
guide me in your truth and teach me,
for you are God my Savior,
and my hope is in you all day long.
Psalm 25:4-5

Jesus told his followers that the day would come when his followers would no longer see him but that "the Counselor, the Holy Spirit...will teach you all things." (John 14:26)

Prayer is sometimes the experience of being taught by God. Our part in this kind of prayer is to let ourselves be humble, curious and teachable. Our part is to let go of the idea that we have the ability to figure things out on our own, that we already have the answers, that we already know what we need to know. Our part is to invite and keep inviting the Spirit to teach us, correct us and guide us, realizing that our knowledge and understanding are limited.

It is a remarkable thing to think about God as our Teacher. It is an even more remarkable reality to experience God as our Teacher.

Many of us struggle to believe that God loves us. We may believe that God is a God of love, but find that we do not trust that God loves us in any personal or meaningful way. Perhaps we feel invisible, insignificant, abandoned.

What we can do is to ask the Spirit to teach us. We can ask the Spirit to teach us that we are loved. Day after day we can pray this prayer and watch and wait for answers. Over time, they will come. In surprising, powerful, life changing ways the Spirit will teach us, show us, and allow us to experience God's love.

The teaching may come directly from whispers of the Spirit to our spirits. Sometimes it will come through Scripture or other reading. Sometimes it will come through experiences of grace in relationships.

We can become students in the school of our loving Creator. The Spirit will teach our hearts to know and to rest in God's unfailing, tender, personal, powerful love for us. On a daily basis we can invite the Spirit to be our Teacher. We can invite God to show us whatever God wants to show us. We can invite God to correct us and guide us.

"Teach, me Lord," we pray with the psalmist, "teach me, for you are my God, my hope, my salvation, my life."

Be my teacher.
Teach me your ways.
Open my heart to your love.
Show me the truth of who you are.
Give me a humble, teachable spirit.
May I watch and listen
for your teaching,
your guidance,
your instruction.

Prayer suggestion:

Invite the Spirit to teach you in specific ways about whatever it is that you need to learn at this time in your life.

Ask God to give you a humble, teachable spirit.

Prayer as Resting in God's Love

Sometimes prayer involves ceasing from all activity. It is coming to an end of effort. Sometimes prayer is resting. In the dynamic interplay of any close relationship there are times of talking, times of listening, and times of simply being together in the ease and comfort that flow out of the safety of loving and being loved.

The prayer of resting in God's love is sometimes experienced in moments of solitude and quietness. And sometimes this prayer is experienced in an inner quietness that we carry with us into the demands of the day.

We are loved. Beyond our imaginings. Beyond telling. Our Maker loves us, delights in us, stays close to us. We are loved by God with a love that is patient, kind, forgiving, full of grace. We are loved by God with a love that values us deeply. We are loved by God with a love that is gentle, humble, tender, self giving, powerful. To take this in, to let this reality change us deeply, we need to crawl into the arms of this Love over and over again and rest.

It turns out that resting is not easy for us. Our anxiety drives us to move, to act, to do something. The gift of arriving at a place where we are able to cease from striving, where we let go of trying to be in charge, where we give up our efforts to try to measure up, can only come to us slowly. Bit by bit God opens us to receive the love poured out for us. Bit by bit we let go of our anxiety. Bit by bit we lean into trust, we learn to surrender ourselves to the arms of Love.

Rest. No words, no particular thoughts, no effort. Safe. Held. Quieted.

Rest. Our heart at home in God.

Trusting as Prayer

But I trust in your unfailing love.
Psalm 13:5

Prayer is an act of trust. More specifically, it is an act of trusting God's unfailing love. Trust is the act of relying on something or someone. When we take the risk of crossing the river by driving over a bridge, we are trusting the bridge to do what it promises to do. We trust the bridge to assist us, to support us, to be there for us. In the same way, to pray is to trust that God will be faithful to God's promises to lovingly care for us and to be with us.

This does not mean that we have to try to conjure up great faith in order to pray. It does not mean we need to pretend to trust when we are in the throws of despair or doubt. It does not mean that we should force ourselves to trust when our capacity to trust seems broken.

The reality is that many of us have a weakened—or even broken—capacity to trust. We may have been significantly hurt or disappointed in close relationships in the past. As a result, we may find it difficult to trust others or God. The possibility of "unfailing love," even of God's unfailing love, may seem like something that is too much to hope for.

So, how can we pray if to pray is to trust and our capacity to trust is weak or broken? Jesus taught his followers that if they had faith as small as a tiny mustard seed, they could move mountains. Perhaps we can think of prayer, then, as an act of taking the tiny mustard seed of faith that we have been given and planting it in the soil of God's faithful love, even as we are honest about our doubts and fears.

In this way, prayer is an act of turning to the One who claims to be the God of loving kindness, and engaging honestly with God—even when our capacity for trust is small. This means that there will be times that our relationship with God will be from a place of doubt or protest. Psalm 13 is just this kind of engagement with God. Most of the psalm is a lament. The Psalmist asks God: "How long will you forget me? How long will you hide your face from me?" It is only at the end of the Psalm that the psalmist says, "But I trust in your unfailing love."

The psalmist pours out his honest lament. It is this honesty that opens the way for the psalmist to remember and trust God's unfailing love. In fact, the lament itself is an act of trusting God's unfailing love. It is a cry of longing for God, of needing God, of feeling separated from God. The cry itself is a mustard seed of hope that, in spite of how things appear, God may be lovingly present through it all.

When we pray we are using the mustard seed of faith we have been given. We are opening ourselves up in some measure to the God who hears and sees and cares about us with intimate, tender, unfailing love. We are trusting, even if in the smallest way, that no matter what our circumstances, in spite of our fears and doubts, that God is with us, enfolding us in Love that is unshakeable.

Sometimes my trust
in your unfailing love
is as small as the smallest seed.
Sometimes I am afraid that you do not love me,
that you are disappointed with me,
that you are impossible to please,
that you are not there for me.
And when life is hard
I sometimes find it difficult to trust that you are with me
and that your love for me is unshakable.
In turning to you today,
I am planting my small seed of faith.
May my trust in your unfailing love
take root and grow.
May I be able one day to fully trust
in your unfailing love.

Prayer suggestion:

As you breathe deeply and easily, let yourself sense God's tender, faithful love enfolding you. Plant your mustard seed of trust in God's unfailing love by telling God your fears, your needs, your doubts, your longings. Then allow yourself to rest quietly in the presence of God's love.

Experiencing Solitude as Prayer

Immediately Jesus made the disciples get into the boat and
go on ahead of him to the other side, while he dismissed
the crowd. After he had dismissed them, he went up on a
mountainside by himself to pray.
Matthew 14: 22-23

Sometimes prayer is a kind of solitude. It is allowing ourselves to be alone with God. According to the Gospels, Jesus went out of his way to find solitude. Sometimes he got up before dawn, sometimes he sent his disciples and the crowds away in the middle of a day of teaching and healing. Many of us find it difficult to make solitude this kind of priority. Getting up early, or saying 'no' to someone in need, or taking a break from working in order to have time alone with God, all of this feels challenging.

Our difficulties with solitude may be in part because we find our sense of value in doing and tasking—rather than in rest. It may be because we tend to under value the gifts that solitude offers. It may be because it is hard to say 'no' to others. It may be because we tend to avoid facing ourselves—our feelings, our failings, our needs—and we expect that solitude might allow these things to surface.

Even if we do finally arrive at a time and a place for solitude we may notice that we still have a huge crowd of people in our heads—a kind of inner chorus that intrudes on our solitude. Sometimes these inner chorus members are our harshest and least grace-full critics. It is possible to sit alone in a quiet room and still be consumed with this kind of inner distraction. And sadly, it can keep us from being present to God and to knowing God as present with us.

One of the gifts of solitude is the clarity it brings about these inner voices and the opportunities it provides to allow the Spirit to help us replace the voices that shame and discourage us with the Voice of love and grace.

The prayer of solitude is time alone with God in which we open our hearts and minds to God, rest in God's love for us and seek God's loving will for our lives. It is a time to listen, to rest in God, to return to the Source of our life.

Sometimes our times of solitude will come in twenty minute chunks of time. Sometimes we might enjoy the luxury of a weekend retreat. Sometimes solitude might be those first waking moments before we get out of bed in the morning, or those last moments before we sleep. Or those minutes alone in our car. Where ever and whenever we find our times of solitude, may we seek and enjoy the rich gifts that times of solitude with God offers us.

I long for time alone with You.

But so much gets in the way.

The urgent.

The necessary things.

And the chorus in my head.

Help me to let go of the chorus members

who are not able to sing in the key of Grace.

Help me to find new chorus members

whose silence can be trusted to be respectful silence.

When you say it is the time for silence

—respectful grace-full silence—

I want the choir to follow your lead.

You, God, be the director of my inner choir.

Help me to say "yes" to times alone with you

so that I may enjoy the rich gift

of resting in your loving Presence.

Prayer suggestion;

When and where can you carve out time to be alone with God? What barriers are you aware of?

Ask God to help you find times of solitude. Plan times of solitude into your schedule.

As soon as you can, spend some time in solitude with God.

Being Still as Prayer

Be still and know that I am God.
Psalm 46:10

Many of us are in motion much of the time. We are in motion at our jobs, in motion with our many activities, in motion seeking entertainment and diversion. Even when we are not in motion physically, we are likely to be in motion mentally. Our minds spin with lists of things to do, with conversations we intend to have, with anxieties that won't go away.

Much of this motion is an inescapable part of life. But it is not the essence of life. There is a time for being in motion. And there is also a time to be still.

"Be still and know that I am God," we read. What is the relationship between being still and knowing that God is God?

Too often the constant physical and mental activities in which we engage are attempts to distract ourselves from the pain in our lives and in our world. We keep ourselves busy as a way of numbing ourselves from the things that overwhelm us.

Our constant motion may also come from a sense of drivenness. We live as if everything depends on our efforts. We act as if we have to try harder and try our hardest. We fall into the trap of believing that we have to figure everything out so that we can somehow change things that are beyond our control. We forget that life is meant to be lived in reliance on God. We forget that God is God and we are not.

To be still is to intentionally let go, for a time, of all our doing, trying and striving. To be still is to allow ourselves to intentionally rest in God's loving presence.

Centering prayer offers a helpful approach to finding stillness in the midst of life. The method is simple, yet it requires much practice because it turns out that it is not easy to still either our bodies or our minds.

This way of praying begins by sitting with feet flat on the floor, our back supported, our breathing slow and easy. And then, gently, introducing a word to serve as a centering point. Just one word of our choosing (like peace, Lord, or Love). The word is not a word to meditate on or to focus on, but a word that we come back to over and over again, every time our mind is distracted. The word is used as a way of expressing our intention to rest in God's loving presence, with minds and bodies that are still.

This prayer of stilling our body and mind allows us to be present to the presence of God. It allows us to cease our striving and to know that God is God. The goal of this kind of prayer is not mindlessness but a focused openness to God. It is a conscious offering of ourselves to God.

I do and do
and strive and strive
and try to figure things out,
forgetting that life
was meant to be lived
in reliance on you.
Help me to still my body
and my mind
so that I can rest
in your presence,
so that I can know again
that you are God.

Prayer suggestion:

Set a timer for twenty minutes (the first few times you might want to begin with ten minutes). Sit comfortably and well supported. Take a few deep easy breaths. Continue breathing slowing and easily. Choose a centering word (Lord, rest, peace, or love are a few examples.) Use this word as an expression of your intention to let go of distractions as they come, and to instead rest in God's loving presence. Continue to gently reintroduce the word each time your mind wanders. Let yourself be still and know that God is God.

Being Quiet as Prayer

In repentance and rest is your salvation,
in quietness and trust is your strength.
Isaiah 30:15

This text from Isaiah is about a time when the Israelites were being pursued by enemies but were refusing God's help. The text tells us that God was full of compassion and ready to help, but they would have none of it.

This is not that different from how we sometimes live our lives. We face problems, even overwhelming challenges, yet we act like we are strong enough and smart enough to handle it on our own. We act as if we don't need God. And we act as if God were not compassionate, as if God were not available, as if God were not willing to help us.

When we finally turn from our self-reliance, rest from our striving and practice prayers of quietness and trust, we find the help and strength we need.

The prayer of quiet is a prayer that makes room for God's presence. When we are quiet, we have come to the end of talking, finished being in charge, finished insisting on our own way. We are ready to make room for God's voice, for God's guidance, for God's way.

The prayer of quiet involves listening and waiting. This often does not feel like prayer. Because we tend to think of prayer as doing something, rather than as waiting quietly before God.

Sue Monk Kid describes an experience of prayer as quietly waiting like this:

> Why couldn't I pray? Why? I stood by the doors, watching the fog, everything in me hushed and unmoving. All at

once I caught my reflection in the glass. I saw my posture silhouetted against the darkness. And it came to me in one of those grace-full moments....I was seeing myself at prayer. I was praying. My still heart, my silence, the very posture of waiting against the backdrop of darkness was my prayer (Sue Monk Kid, *When the Heart Waits*, HarperSanFrancisco, 1990. pp. 125-126.)

When we move away from all the noise and move into a place of quiet, a space is opened in our hearts. There is room in the quietness for God's Spirit to move, to heal, to guide, and to speak. We discover that we are not alone. We discover that we can trust in the goodness and presence of God.

This is counter intuitive for many of us. We tend to trust that all our activity will help us and strengthen us. And we tend to believe that God expects us to be in constant motion. During life's difficulties and crises being quiet is often the last thing we think to do. But God calls to us, "Turn to me, rest in my care, quiet yourself and trust me, this will be your salvation, this will be your strength."

I have come to an end
of being in charge,
I have come to an end
of my own efforts.
I have no more words.

I come to you
to rest in quiet before you,
to entrust all the concerns of my heart
to your loving care.
I seek your voice,
your will, your way.
Give me the grace to
quiet myself before you.

Prayer suggestion:

Practice another session of Centering Prayer. Set a timer for twenty minutes. Sit comfortably and well supported. Take a few deep easy breaths. Continue breathing slowly and easily. Choose a word to center your thoughts (Lord, rest, peace, or love are a few examples.) Use this word as an expression of your intention to let go of distractions as they come, and to instead rest in God's loving presence. Continue to reintroduce the word each time your mind wanders. Let yourself be still and quiet before God, resting in God's unfailing love.

Releasing our Burdens as Prayer

Come to me, all you who are weary and burdened,
and I will give you rest.
Take my yoke upon you and learn of me,
for I am gentle and humble in heart
and you will find rest for your souls.
Matthew 11:28-29

Prayer begins, not with our call to God, but with God's call to us. "Come to me," Jesus calls. "Come." All our praying is in some way a response to God's initiative. But we may misunderstand the invitation God extends. We may not hear it as the call of Love. We may suspect that if we respond to this call, we will be met with shame, with rejection or with impossible demands. As a result, we may hesitate to respond at all. Or we may go to God in prayer but full of a need to prove ourselves, driven by fears that even in prayer we need to work hard and look good.

When we listen carefully to the invitation that is extended we hear something surprising. "Come to me and rest," Jesus calls. "I know you are weary and burdened. I am gentle and humble, so you will find that you are safe with me. I love you. You will find that you can completely, fully rest with me, knowing you are loved, knowing you are safe."

Jesus acknowledges our weariness. Jesus knows we are burdened. Jesus knows we need to rest. And Jesus tells us that it is possible to rest with him because he is gentle and humble. When we respond to Jesus' call, we will not be met with demands or shame or judgment. We will be met with compassion. We will be held in arms of love.

Prayer is a response to God's initiative, to God's invitation to come and rest. Prayer is rest in the deepest sense of the word—rest for our souls.

When we rest we stop all doing, all proving, all effort. We can be done with our striving, with our self-reliance, with our pretense, with our heavy load. We can release all that burdens our heart to God's loving care and rest in God's loving presence.

This promise of rest to which Jesus calls us is an echo of the same promise made centuries earlier by the psalmist who described God as our loving Shepherd. We have read or heard this promise many times, but we tend to read right past it. "The Lord is my Shepherd I shall not be in want. He makes me lie down in green pastures, he leads me beside quiet waters. He restores my soul." The Shepherd provides rest.

Prayer is resting in the green pastures and beside the quiet waters of God's love. Prayer is resting in God's love, experiencing the gentleness and humility of Jesus. Prayer is rest for our souls.

You call to me
to come to you
and rest.
It is the last thing
I imagined you would say
or want from me.
You surprise me
with you gentleness
your humility
your kindness
your love.
Grant me the ability to rest in your presence.
May I find rest
for my soul.

Prayer suggestion:

Sit quietly in prayer. Ask God to help you rest in the green pastures and beside the quiet waters of God's love for you. Ask God to help you respond to Jesus' call to come to him and rest. Sit still and quiet for a time, resting in God's tender love for you.

Letting Ourselves Be Carried as Prayer

*Some men came, bringing to him a paralytic, carried by
four of them. Since they could not get him to Jesus because
of the crowd, they made an opening in the roof above Jesus
and, after digging through it,
lowered the mat the paralyzed man was lying on.*
Mark 2:3-4

Sometimes prayer is letting ourselves be carried by others.
Sometimes we cannot pray. We may try to talk with God, or
to listen to God, but find that we are unable to even begin. We
may be too sick physically to pray. Or we may be too depressed
or overwhelmed to pray. Or we may be in too much spiritual
distress.

There are times when we are the paralytic. We cannot walk.
And if Jesus came to a nearby neighborhood there would be no
way that we could get ourselves there to ask him to heal us. We
would have to let ourselves be carried to Jesus.

Most of us have experienced times when we were unable
to pray. Times when we are too sick, or too exhausted, or too
discouraged, or too overwhelmed. We may go from times of
trying to please God by praying good enough and hard enough,
to times when we find ourselves unable to pray at all. Surpris-
ingly, the times when we are unable to pray can become times of
experiencing grace.

Periods of not being able to pray put us in the position of the
paralyzed man in this story from Mark's Gospel. We need help
and healing, but we cannot bring ourselves to Jesus. We need
our friends and loved ones to carry us. We need to be carried
on the stretcher of the love and prayer of others. Our prayer in
such times is to lie on the stretcher and let ourselves rest in the
experience of being carried by others.

Sometimes, when we find ourselves in the position of the paraplegic, the distress we are already experiencing is compounded by the spiritual shame we feel for not being able to pray. But this spiritual shame is not necessary. We can let it go.

When we cannot pray, we can ask for prayer from others and let our prayer be the grace of being carried by others' prayers directly into the loving arms of Jesus.

There are times when I cannot pray.
Times when I am too sick,
or too discouraged.
Remind me that there is no
shame in this.
Help me to remember that this is not
a sign of spiritual failure.
Give me the grace
in those times to let my prayer
be the prayer of the paralytic.
Give me the grace
to be carried
by other peoples' loving prayers
on my behalf.

Prayer suggestion:

Reflect on a time when you were unable pray. What was your experience at that time? Ask God to show you if there is some way in which you need to allow yourself to be carried by the prayers of others in the present. If so, call, text or email a few trusted friends and ask them to pray for you. Allow yourself to be carried by their prayers.

Prayer as Receiving from God

Too often we think of prayer as another hoop to jump through, another requirement to figure out, another obligation, another thing to check off our to-do list. But prayer is pure gift. It is the breathing in of the Life of our Maker. It is the embrace of Love. It is the experience of opening our hands and hearts to receive the outpouring of gift upon gift from the Giver of all good gifts. It is the experience of receiving from God.

How is it that such good news is not easy for us? What happened to our innocent, childlike capacity for receiving?

Over time our open hands have closed into fists. Our hearts have become walled fortresses. Fear, anger, and despair have convinced us that we must fend for ourselves. We have closed and braced ourselves against the danger.

God knows. God understands our dilemma. God pursues, waits, knocks, waits some more. All the time God is pouring out good gifts. All the time God is pouring out God's heart, God's Self to us.

"Receive," God whispers. "Let me remove one brick from your fortress. Let me help you unclench one finger. Let me put one drop of honey on your lips. I am Life. I am Love. I long to fill you full to overflowing."

Prayer is grace opening our clenched hands and hearts. It is God wooing us to consent to receive the joy, the peace, the fullness of life and love that is being offered to us every moment of every day.

Receiving as Prayer

Every good and perfect gift is from above,
coming down from the Father of the heavenly lights
who does not change like shifting shadows.
James 1:17

This text reveals some remarkable truths about God. God is the Giver of every good and perfect gift. And God is the "Father of heavenly lights who does not change like shifting shadows." These images are powerful, beautiful, surprising, stunning.

God is the Giver of all that is good. God gives. We receive. This is the structure of reality. Our life, our breath, everything we have, we have received from God.

A vital part of what it means to pray is not only to express our needs to God, but to actively receive God's good gifts.

It turns out that this is not so easy. What comes naturally to a young child being cared for by loving parents does not come naturally to us in our relationship with God. For one thing, we often get confused in our thinking and try to turn the structure of the universe upside down. We imagine that God needs us to give and give and do and do. We imagine that it is not us, but God, who needs to do all the receiving.

Perhaps our thinking about this becomes confused because of fear. Some of us live with the fear that God does not really love or value us. This fear blocks our capacity to receive the good gifts God gives. Some of us may have difficulty receiving from God because we fear that we do not deserve good things—not spiritually, relationally or materially. Or we may fear that, rather than being the Giver of all that is good, God instead is cruel and unkind. Fears and distortions about ourselves and about God make it difficult for us to freely receive the good gifts God gives.

But God does not waver. God keeps giving all that is good. And all the time that God is pouring out good gifts into our lives God is also working to free us from the fears that block our ability to receive. Writer and theologian George MacDonald describes it like this:

> There are good things God must delay giving, until his child has a pocket to hold them—until God gets his child to make that pocket. God must first make him fit to receive and to have. There is no part of our nature that shall not be satisfied—and that not by lessening it, but by enlarging it to embrace an ever-enlarging enough. (George MacDonald, *Discovering the Character of God* compiled by Michael R. Phillips [Minneapolis: Bethany House Publishers 1989], p. 156).

God not only offers us good gifts. God also helps us to grow in our capacity to receive these gifts. Prayer is receiving good gifts from God who is the Giver of all that is good. Prayer is also the process by which God helps us increase our capacity to receive these gifts.

May God grant us the grace to make pockets to hold God's good gifts. May we receive more and more of all that God desires to give.

You are the Giver of every good gift.
You are the Love behind every good gift.
The air I breathe, the food I eat,
the shelter where I rest and work,
the companionship I enjoy,
the hope that comes,
the peace that protects,
the joy that surprises.
You give and give and give.
You are the Giver of every good gift.
I receive and receive again from your loving hand.
Open my eyes,
open my heart,
open my hands,
to receive all your good gifts.

Prayer suggestion:

List some of the many good gifts you are being given. Picture these gifts falling gently down to you, poured out by God who loves you. Open your hands and heart to receive all you are being given.

Receiving Grace as Prayer

For we do not have a high priest who is unable
to sympathize with our weaknesses,
but we have one who has been tempted in every way,
just as we are—yet was without sin.
Let us then approach the throne of grace with confidence,
so that we may receive mercy and
find grace to help us in our time of need.
Hebrews 4:15-16

Prayer is receiving mercy and grace to help us in our time of need. This text reminds us that God, in Jesus, knows what it is like to live with human limits and weaknesses. God, in Jesus, knows and sympathizes with us when we struggle, when we are tempted, when we fail. Because of this, we can trust that when we pray in the midst of our temptations and failings, we will be met with compassion, mercy and grace.

Our temptations are many. We are tempted by fear, by despair, by self-reliance and self-serving. We are tempted by pride and greed. We are tempted by self loathing and self harm. We are tempted by the drive to control what is beyond our control. We are tempted to go our own way. We are tempted by all of these and many other forms of closing our hearts to the love of God and to loving our neighbor as ourselves.

When we are struggling and failing it is easy to think that we need to hide from God. Maybe we need to sort things out and get ourselves back on track before we pray. The reason we find this reaction almost instinctive is that we imagine that God responds to less than perfect people with anger, disappointment and condemnation. We forget that God sympathizes with us in our weakness. We forget that God has promised to receive our prayers with mercy and with grace.

263

What does it mean to find mercy and grace? It means that when we pray in our struggles, our brokenness, our sin and failings God will welcome us, embrace us, and offer us understanding and kindness. It means that God's love for us is unfailing. It means that God's love for us and valuing of us does not waver or change, no matter what we have done or not done.

God is a good and loving parent whose patience and kindness and delight in us far exceeds that of the most loving biological parent. God responds to us with a tender heart and an eagerness to help. There is no need for shame about our weaknesses with God. God knows. God, in Jesus, understands what it is to be human. God welcomes us and all our weaknesses with open arms.

The amazing gift of prayer is that when we share the reality of our weaknesses with God it becomes an opportunity for greater intimacy, affection and joy between us. Go to God with any need, any weakness, any temptation, any failing. You will find mercy. You will find help. You will find grace.

I am tempted every day
with greed and pride and self-serving,
with fear and despair and self-reliance.
I am weak.
I need your help.
I am in awe that when I come to you
with my weakness and temptations and failings
you greet me with such tenderness,
such kindness, such patience,
such empathy.
You are merciful and full of grace.
Your mercy and grace heal me and help me.
Thank you.

Prayer suggestion:

Talk with God about your weaknesses and temptations. Let yourself know God's empathy and understanding. Allow yourself to receive God's mercy, help and grace. Listen. God may have something to say.

Receiving Peace as Prayer

Peace I leave with you; my peace I give you. I do not
give to you as the world gives. Do not let your hearts be
troubled and do not be afraid.
John 14:27

Prayer is receiving the gift of peace from the One who is the
Prince of Peace. Jesus offered his disciples the gift of peace
just hours before he was arrested and crucified. His followers
were about to experience the darkest days of their lives. All
hope was about to be crushed. All they had given their lives
to was about to be lost. Their own lives would feel threatened.
And the man they had come to love and trust would be taken
from them.

Jesus was aware of this dark night they were all about to enter.
Jesus knew their hearts were about to be deeply troubled and
that they were all about to be terrified. The gift of peace that
Jesus offered them did not spare his followers from experiencing
the coming distress. But his words planted a seed.

Jesus speaks into our lives in this same way. When life as we
know it is in some way threatened, when we are full of anxiety
and despair, Jesus speaks his peace into our hearts and minds.

People sometimes talk about experiences of being surprised
by this gift of peace in times of crisis. Times when life as they
knew it was threatened. Times when they had no idea what
was ahead. In the middle of deeply troubled times, anxious and
afraid, peace can come as a pure gift. We don't expect to experience
peace in times like that. But the moments of peace during
these times can be some of the sweetest peace we have ever
known.

The gift of peace is not under our control. It may not be

constant. But it comes, a surprising gift, again and again. It is a gift that carries us on gentle wings. It is a gift that touches the deepest parts of our spirit.

Peace is a gift that we are offered every day. Even when we are in a crisis. Even when we are facing loss and death. And even in the ordinary moments of ordinary days. Jesus stands before us and speaks his peace to us "My peace I give to you."

Allowing ourselves to hear those words and to open our hearts and minds to receive this extraordinary gift of peace is a form of prayer.

Prince of Peace,
You stand before me
offering peace.
It is beyond understanding.
How can your peace calm my fears?
How can your tranquility replace my anxiety?
Grant me the grace to hear your offer.
Let it sink deep within me,
down to the places where my fears have their roots.
That is where I need your peace to grow.
Grant me the grace
to receive your peace.

Prayer suggestion:

Sit quietly, breathing deeply and easily. Read this text aloud slowly. Receive them as Jesus' words to you personally. "My peace I give to you." Sit in silence with these words for a few minutes and read them again. Breathe in this gift of peace. Receive this gift of peace today.

Receiving Wisdom as Prayer

If any of you lacks wisdom, he should ask God, who gives generously to all without finding fault, and it will be given to him...The wisdom that comes from heaven is first of all pure; then peace-loving, considerate, submissive, full of mercy, and good fruit, impartial and sincere.
James 1:5, 3:17

We are invited by this text to ask God for wisdom. We are told that we will receive wisdom from God. God will "give generously to all without finding fault." We will not be shamed or judged for our need. We will not have to jump through hoops to have this need met. God will be generous with us, giving us an abundance of the wisdom we seek.

But what exactly are we seeking when we ask for wisdom? What is wisdom? According to the book of Proverbs, wisdom is a clear understanding of what is right and just and fair. But Proverbs takes us even deeper, telling us that wisdom is a way of life that is marked by reliance on and deep reverence for our Maker (Proverbs 3:5,6).

This text from the book of James tells us more specifically what wisdom from God looks like when it is lived out. We are told that it is pure. Wisdom is a single-minded intention to follow God's guidance for our lives. It is peace-loving, considerate, full of mercy, impartial and sincere. This description matches closely the description of love found in I Corinthians 13.

When we ask for wisdom from God, we will receive a life transforming gift. We will be given the gift of being able to listen less to all the confusing, conflicting voices in our heads and in our world so that we can listen more to the voice of Love. We will begin to let go of all that creates conflict within and without and we will learn to practice the way of peace. And we will begin to be more and more considerate, respectful, impartial and genuine in our treatment of and interactions with others.

As wisdom enters our hearts and minds and is lived out in our lives we will be transformed. We will become more and more like Jesus, more and more like the God of Love that Jesus came to show us.

Wisdom is not simply about making good decisions. Wisdom is about God's mind and heart becoming our own. To ask for wisdom is to let go of relying on our own ideas and to surrender in joy to the wisdom God offers.

God longs to give us this wisdom generously, abundantly. God longs to fill us full of this wisdom which is God's life in us and through us.

You, God, are all wisdom,
you are peace-loving,
merciful, considerate and
full of loving kindness.
I ask for your wisdom today.
Thank you for your promise
to give to all who ask.
Thank you for your promise to give generously,
without finding fault.
Teach me your ways.
Let me know your heart
and mind.
I ask for your wisdom, God.

Prayer suggestion:

What are you feeling uncertain about at this time? Ask God for the wisdom you need today.

At the end of the day, review your sense of ways in which God guided you or filled you with wisdom.

Receiving a New Heart as Prayer

I will give you a new heart
and put a new spirit in you;
I will remove from you your heart of stone
and give you a heart of flesh.
Ezekiel 36:26

Prayer is allowing God to radically change us. God is the One we speak to, listen to, worship, serve and rest with as we pray. Over time, in these encounters, God begins to change our heart. Our heart of stone is softened, broken open and replaced with a heart of flesh. Hearts of flesh are hearts that are vulnerable. Unlike hearts of stone which are defended and well protected, hearts of flesh can feel both pain and joy.

Because flesh hearts can feel pain, we often find ourselves wondering if we would be better off with a stone heart. We do not like to be vulnerable. But there is no other way to experience love. Love is vulnerable. Love lays down its protection. Love exposes its tender longing for respectful intimacy. Love grieves with those who grieve, rejoices with those who rejoice and cares for one's neighbor as oneself.

Our vulnerable longing to give and receive love is the deepest truth of all about who we are. This longing exists in each one of us. It is this tender, powerful longing that God desires to unearth in us. It is to awaken and free this longing that God offers to replace our stone hearts with hearts of flesh.

The miracle of this heart transplant—this radical change in us—takes place as we are exposed to God's love, to God's vulnerability toward us. God expresses a vulnerable longing for intimacy with us. God seeks us out. God calls to us. God invites us. God risks our unresponsiveness, tolerates our hesitations, refuses to give up on us. And, over time, we begin to experience our vulnerability in a different way. We see the flesh-hearted life for what it is: a life of Love.

It is in repeated encounters with God's vulnerable, active love that our own hearts begin to soften and break open.

You gazed at me,
inviting me to gaze back into the ocean of your love.
It was unbearable.
I could not sustain a gaze at first.
Only glances.
Your love fell in waves against my shame and fear and pride,
carrying away small segments at a time.
It felt like certain death.
And so it was.
Little by little I died.
I thought there would be nothing left.
But you knew the seed of life you had once formed in me
would lie exposed, aching with love and longing.
And so I was.
I was unearthed
by your loving gaze.
You treated me as though I were the pearl of great price
that you had sold everything to buy.
And so you had.

Prayer suggestion:

Invite God to give you a heart transplant. Offer to God your defended, well-protected heart. Ask God to expose your tender heart of flesh.

Receiving God as Prayer

God is love.
Whoever lives in love
lives in God,
and God in him.
I John 4:16

The most important gift that anyone can ever give us is the gift of themselves. More than anything else, children need their parents to give themselves in love to them. They need their parents to breathe life into them. To see them and know them and guide them and care for them. To teach them and nurture them. To pour their lives and love into them.

God, our true Parent, the Giver of every good and perfect gift, gives this most important gift of all to us. God gives God's Self to us in love.

In the Genesis story of creation we read that human life begins with the breath of God. And so it is, every day, every breath we breathe, we are breathing in the life of God which has been breathed out to us.

The Gospels continue this understanding of God. The Gospels tell the story of God coming to us in Jesus. Jesus was Immanuel, God with us. The healing life of Jesus was God-in-flesh, giving God's Self to us. And then, most astonishing of all, in Christ's death God poured out the loving heart of God to all. God poured out grace, forgiveness, mercy, hope and the life of God to us all.

And so it is that every day, every moment, God pours out God's Self to us. God gives it all away. Flowing from the heart of God is all the goodness and kindness and love and mercy and forgiveness that are the life of God.

Our part is to receive. Our part is to breathe in the breath of God and live—to say "Yes" to God and receive the life and love of God, to invite God to live in us so that we might live in God so that we might live in love, which is life itself.

The heart of all prayer, of all living, is this: receiving God.

When we receive the gift of the other, whether human or divine, we receive by opening our hearts in love. We receive the love of another by giving our heart—our love—in return.

May we receive the gift of our loving God more fully each day. May this be our prayer.

You give yourself to me.
You pour yourself,
Grace, Love, Life,
Light, Peace, Joy.
Your pour yourself out to me, into me, through me.
My heart's desire
is to receive you,
to be home to you.
Grant me the grace
to receive the gift of you
more and more each day.

Prayer suggestion:

Invite God to make your heart soft, open, ready to receive the gift of God.

Sit quietly, breathing slowly, easily.

See the Light of God's love surrounding you and filling you.

Allow yourself to receive this gift of God, allow yourself to be filled with Love.

Prayer as Transformation

When we breathe in the breath of God, we live. When we consent to more of God—allowing God to empty us of pride and deceit, of self-reliance and self-serving—we are made ready to receive Love. The more we consent and empty, the more we receive. And the more we receive, the more we are changed. We become home to more of God, home to more of Love.

Prayer is this path of transformation. Prayer brings us into conscious contact with our Maker. We encounter Love. We are awed, confronted, corrected, healed, forgiven, freed, blessed, sent out to be a blessing.

Prayer changes us in radical ways. We may not look more religious. But we will begin to look more real. More present. More open. More receptive. More compassionate. More peaceful. More loving.

The change that God is ready to do in us is astounding. Scripture tells us that the transformation that God desires to do in us is to make us more and more like Christ. We might want to consider if we are willing to invite this kind of transformation. Is this the way we want our characters to be shaped? Like Christ's?

Are we ready to be changed to be like the Man who gave everything away, including his life? The person who was always outside the box? The Healer who described himself as gentle and humble? The One who lived in full joyful surrender to the Father?

This is the transformation to which God calls us. This is the journey of prayer.

Being Empty as Prayer

Blessed are the poor in spirit,
for theirs is the kingdom of God.
Matthew 5:3

We tend to come to God full of ourselves. Full of pride, full of a need to "get it right", full of a need to prove ourselves, full of self-reliance.

But prayer is not about all we have done, or all we believe, or all the ways we work to prove ourselves. Prayer is coming to God empty of all of this. Prayer is coming to God with empty hands, ready to receive, ready to be helped, ready to be changed, ready to be filled.

Kathleen Norris in her book *Meditations on Mary* wrote about her reflections on the message of the Magnificat. The Magnificat is the hymn that was sung by Mary to her cousin Elizabeth. In this hymn Mary sings praise to God because he "has brought down the powerful from their thrones, and lifted up the lowly; has filled the hungry with good things, and sent the rich away empty" (Luke 1: 52-53). This is how Kathleen reflects on these words:

> How rich had I been that day, how full of myself? Too full
> to recognize need and hunger, my own and anyone else's?
> So powerfully providing for myself that I couldn't admit my
> need for help of others? Too busy to know a blessing when
> it came to me? (Kathleen Norris, *Meditations on Mary*.
> Viking Studio,New York, 1999. pg14).

According to Jesus, the kingdom of God does not belong to those who have achieved spiritual success of some kind. Rather, the kingdom belongs to those who know their need, who know their poverty, who do not hide their emptiness. When we realize our spiritual poverty, our need, our emptiness, we come to God in a spirit of honesty and humility. We are teachable. We are open. We are receptive.

Jesus taught his disciples to "abide in him" like the branch abides with the vine. In other words, Jesus taught his disciples to draw their life from him. When we believe that God expects us to be the vine, or out of our own pride we try to be the vine rather than the branch, we end up becoming defensive and exhausted. But when we allow ourselves to be the branch and know our need for the life that comes only from the vine, we can live humbly.

The kingdom of God is available to us when we are emptied of our attempts to prove ourselves, when we are done with our spiritual pride, when we let ourselves be poor in spirit. Prayer is being empty, ready to receive.

I come to you

empty and poor.

I release to you all my spiritual pride.

Allow me to be what I truly am,

a branch

in need of the life that flows

from the vine.

May my poverty of spirit

be the opportunity for your blessing.

May I receive your life,

your kingdom.

Prayer suggestion:

Take a few deep breaths. Open your hands. Ask God to help you release all that you hold on to. Ask God to help you entrust all you are and have and care about to God's loving care. See yourself letting go of your pride, self-reliance, self-serving and fear. Surrender all that holds your heart into God's care. Listen as Jesus says to you, "Blessed are the poor in spirit, for theirs is the kingdom of God."

Being Filled as Prayer

Blessed are those who hunger and thirst for righteousness,
for they will be filled.
Matthew 5:6

The word "righteousness" as it is used here refers primarily to a relationship with God. So, when Jesus pronounces blessing on those who hunger and thirst for righteousness, he is speaking of those who hunger and thirst for a relationship with God. Jesus was saying, "You will be blessed when you hunger and thirst for a relationship with God. You will be blessed by being filled with the One for whom you hunger."

When we allow ourselves to experience our hunger for God, we will be filled.

It may not seem like a difficult thing to know that we are hungry for a relationship with God. But it turns out that it is. It turns out that many of us are unaware of our spiritual hunger. Many of us are spiritually anorexic. Physical anorexia is the inability to respond appropriately to the natural hunger our bodies experience for food. Some people can become so anorexic in relationship to food that they do not experience their stomach's growling as hunger, nor do they associate the headache and fatigue they feel when they have gone a long time without food as hunger. Food has, for them, become something dangerous and hunger is seen as frightening. So natural, healthy hunger is denied, even to the point, for some, of death by starvation.

In much the same way we can deny our spiritual hunger. We can experience the natural sensations of our longing for a relationship with God but deny this longing because it feels too frightening. We may be afraid because we don't know where this longing will lead, or we have been fed nothing but spiritual toxins in the past and as a result we fear that there is nothing available that will truly fill our souls. Out of fear of one kind or another we can deny and distract ourselves from our hunger for God, and as a result find that we are starving spiritually.

Simone Weil wrote about this problem in her book *Waiting for God*. "The danger," she writes "is not that the soul should doubt whether there is any bread, but that by a lie, it should persuade itself that it is not hungry."

Jesus spoke of the importance of allowing ourselves to experience our spiritual hunger. It may seem like a vulnerable and risky thing to let ourselves feel our deep hunger for God. But unless we know that we are spiritually hungry, we will not seek nourishment.

Jesus' words of blessing and promise tell us that it is worth the risk. When we allow ourselves to hunger for a relationship with God, we will be fed. There is Bread. God waits to feed us, to fill us.

Prayer is taking the risk to hunger for God. Prayer is allowing ourselves to be filled.

I am afraid to feel my hunger for you
because I don't know if I can ever be filled.
Give me the courage and the hope I need
to experience my hunger for you.
Strengthen me to seek the Bread you offer.
Feed me,
fill me.

Prayer suggestion:

Sit quietly. Take a few deep breaths.

Ask God to show you how you might be avoiding or denying your hunger for God.

Ask God to allow you to experience your spiritual hunger.

Hear Jesus' words of blessing, "Blessed are you when you hunger and thirst for God, for you will be filled."

As you sit quietly, open your hands and wait in silence. Allow God to fill you.

Renewing Our Minds as Prayer

And do not be conformed to this world,
but be transformed by the renewing of your mind.
Romans 12:2

As we move away from prayers that are rote, prayers that are performances, prayers that are attempts to appease or change God and we move into a life of prayer in which we are broken and open hearted, something begins to happen. We begin to encounter God. We begin to experience conscious contact with our Source, our Life. We begin to live in relationship with the God of Love. We are impacted by these encounters—by this Love. We begin to change at a deep level.

Encountering God transforms the way we see ourselves, God and others. Slowly, we who have thought of ourselves as worthless and unlovable, begin to know ourselves as valued and to experience ourselves as loved. We who have defended ourselves with walls of pride and arrogance, learn to live in growing humility and grace. We, who have privately cowered before false gods who are harsh and demanding or distant and uncaring, gradually begin to know the kindness, the tender mercies of the God of Love. And we, who have guarded our hearts from freely loving our neighbor without judgement or fear, begin to see and know others through God's eyes of love.

The condemnation and judgments we hold against ourselves for the ways we have been wounded and the ways we have wounded others begins to ease. The pronouncements against ourselves as failures or less-than or unlovable or not-capable-of-loving lose their power. Our grandiose versions of ourselves fade. Our fears that God will abandon us or reject us or punish us begin to heal. Our anger at others for their neglect or abuse starts to give way to the experience of extending mercy and forgiveness.

It may take many years for God to renew our minds. It may take years for us to come to know in a deep and abiding way that the true story of our lives is that—no matter what has happened to us and no matter what we have done—God was there with us loving us, valuing us.

Prayer is the renewal of our minds. Prayer is our Maker offering us a new way of thinking and knowing that will transform our lives.

You are transforming me.
You are shining the light of your
abiding presence into
the darkest places of my mind.
You are rewriting my story.
You are setting me free
to know your goodness,
to know your tender mercies,
to know myself as loved,
and thus to be capable of loving others.
I am beginning to see that at the heart of prayer
is your Love which transforms me.

Prayer suggestion:

Invite God to do a transforming, renewing work in your mind.

Wait in quiet, asking for the courage and humility to hear and see anything God might want to show you.

Write whatever comes to you and share it with a trusted spiritual friend or advisor.

Softening Our Heart as Prayer

Come, let us bow down in worship,
let us kneel before the Lord our Maker,
for he is our God
and we are the people of his pasture,
the flock under his care.
Today, if you hear his voice,
do not harden your hearts.
Psalm 95:6-8

Our hearts long for God. Yet, too often, we defend ourselves against this longing. We protect our hearts by hardening them against the love we seek because we are afraid that our longings will never be satisfied. To people like us God calls out, "Do not harden your hearts. I am your Maker, your God. You are my people, you are under my care. Listen for my voice. When you hear my voice of love, soften your hearts. Let yourself trust my love and care for you."

Prayer is responding to God's call to soften our hearts.

This 'softening' is not something that happens magically or quickly. It is usually something that happens over time.

It begins as we listen for God's voice of love and notice the extent to which we harden our hearts. Do we hear and see God's love only to push it away by questioning it and ourselves? Do we find ourselves feeling dead or numb inside? If we find that our hearts are hard in these ways, we can ask for the grace to soften our hearts. We can pray for the openness to listen and trust God's voice of love. When we bow before our Maker we can ask that our fearful, hardened hearts be healed. We can ask God to soften our hearts so that they are able to receive the love that God is pouring out to us every day.

Softening our hearts also often requires us to learn to discount other voices that threaten to crowd out God's voice. We hear voices of accusation. Voices of discouragement. Voices of shame. Unfortunately these voices sometimes get our attention more easily than the voice of Love. Even worse, we sometimes believe that these voices are the voice of God. We may actually expect accusation and shame from God. As a result, we may be afraid to listen for God's voice because we may feel we cannot bear any more accusation or shame.

But God's voice of love is not in the voice of accusation. God's voice may speak loving correction—to correct our fears, to correct our self-will and destructive ways, to correct our hard hearts, to correct our refusal to love and be loved. But God's voice is not the voice of an accuser. God's voice is speaking life to us. God is speaking grace to us. God is calling us into loving relationship. This is the voice of God.

When we hear this Voice of loving kindness it is good to ask God to soften our hearts so that we can receive the love for which we have always longed.

I hear your voice—even when there are many other voices.
You are the one saying that I am yours,
That you care for me,
That you love me.
But I feel myself harden
with fear and doubt.
I have trouble trusting your love.
Soften my heart.
Help me to pay attention to
my longing for your love.
Help me to respond to your love
with a soft and joyful heart.

Prayer suggestion:

Read Psalm 95:6-8 several times.

Listen to God's voice of love for you.

Notice your responses. Talk to God about your fears and defenses.

Ask God to soften your heart as you respond to God's voice.

Moving into God's Light as Prayer

I am writing you a new command,
its truth is seen in him and you,
because the darkness is passing
and the true light is already shining.
Anyone who claims to be in the light
but hates his brother is still in the darkness.
Whoever loves his brother lives in the light,
and there is nothing to make him stumble.
I John 2:8-9

When we pray, we open ourselves to God who is light. The thought of this can be frightening at first. We may fear that the light will expose all that is wrong with us in a way that will be condemning or punitive. But as we look more closely at this text, we see that the light of God is the love of God. Moving toward God's light, opening ourselves to God's light in prayer, is a movement out of the darkness and blindness of our hatred, toward the light of God's love.

God's light does indeed expose the darkness that is in us. But not to condemn us. God's light exposes what needs healing and correction in order to free us from our self-serving ways, our defensiveness, our pride, our judgement, our condemnation of ourselves and others. God's light frees us from all that is damaged in us and empowers us to love as God loves.

If our religious pursuits lead us into self righteousness, hardness of heart, judgement and condemnation, we are not moving toward the light of God's love. All of these symptoms are signs that we are still in the darkness. Sometimes, out of fear that God is harsh and condemning, we strive to please and placate an angry, abusive god. We may call this prayer. We may call this right religion. But according to Scripture it is not.

Prayer brings us in humility and growing openness into the presence of our Creator who is light, whose light is the light of love. This is not a God that needs to be placated, but a God who heals us, blesses us, receives us and leads us in the way of love. This is a God who pours out all of who God is to us. As we move into the light of God's love, we are changed, we are released more and more from the darkness of our hatred, we are filled more and more with love.

This was the heart cry of the psalmist in Psalm 4:6: " Let the light of your face shine on us." Free us from the darkness of our hatred, our resentment, our judgement. Remake us with the light of your love. Let the beautiful, healing light of your face shine on us.

I have hatred in my heart.
I am bitter, resentful, judgmental.
I feel entitled to this hardness.
I cling to this darkness.
But it consumes me
and hurts others.
This hatred blocks your Spirit.
It blocks the light of your love
from shining in me
and through me.
Come, Light.
Come, Love.
Shine on me.
Shine in me.
Let the darkness pass,
let your light come.
May I live in the light of your love.

Prayer suggestion:

Ask God to show you where there is darkness in your life. Ask God to reveal whatever hatred, resentment or bitterness exists in you. Invite God to free you from the darkness of your hatred, your resentment, your judgement. Pray that the beautiful, healing light of God's face will shine on you and empower you to move out of the darkness and into the light of God's unfailing love.

Loving our Enemies as Prayer

*"But I tell you who hear me: Love your enemies, do good
to those who hate you, bless those who curse you, pray for
those who mistreat you."*
Luke 6: 27

As we expose our hearts in prayer, our hearts soften in love
and our eyes begin to see life through God's eyes of love.
As a result, we are changing. We are being transformed. We are
being set free to be who God made us to be—people who love
as God loves.

Love moves us beyond ourselves and our circle of family
and friends. Love moves us even to a different relationship
with those whom we have come to see as enemies. People who
hate us, or mistreat us, or curse us, or in some way threaten
us become people that we now know are loved by God. They
become people for whom we are called to pray—people we are
called to treat with kindness and respect.

This call to love our enemies, to pray for them and to do good
to them, is a call to radical change. Our instinct is to judge
those who are unkind to us and to defend ourselves against
them. Our instinct is to see them as less than human, less than
precious, less than people loved by God. We want to return hate
for hate, cursing for cursing, mistreatment for mistreatment. It
seems right. It seems fair. It seems like something we should be
able to do in the name of justice, believing God is on our side.

But this is not the way of Love. This is not God's way. To
pray is to be radically transformed by the God whose essence is
love. To pray is to express this radical transformation by praying
blessing on those who curse us and by being kind to those who
mistreat us.

Nelson Mandela did this. He was imprisoned in South Africa's jails for much of his adult life because he sought political change in his country. In the years that he was held against his will he befriended his guards. He treated them with kindness. He showed them love. This love did not end when he was eventually freed. It did not end when he was made president of his country. He seated these men as guests of honor on the platform when he was sworn into office.

Mandela could have returned hatred for hatred and lived a bitter life. But he extended loving respect to his captors and this changed everything. It kept him grounded in love. And it planted seeds of peace and reconciliation that blossomed into the first fruits of the healing of a nation.

The story of President Mandela stirs something deep in our spirits. It stirs a recognition of who we really are, of who God made us to be, of the love that we are capable of when we allow God to heal us and free us.

Prayer leads to this. Prayer becomes this. It leads to praying for our enemies, to doing good to those who hate us. What might we pray when we pray for our enemies? We might pray for our own eyes and hearts to open in love so that we can see them as valued and loved by God. We might pray for their eyes and hearts to open so that they might know themselves to be loved by their Maker. We might pray for humility and wisdom to know how to be the expression of God's love to them. We might pray for peace, justice and reconciliation to come to them and to us that we might all know together God's healing love.

You know that when someone is unkind to me,
when someone threatens me in any way,
I see them as an enemy.
My instinct is to return hate for hate.
It seems fair to me. It seems appropriate.
I know this leaves me hardened and bitter.
I know it makes reconciliation more difficult.
You call me to love those that hate me,
to pray for those who would harm me.
I will need new eyes and a new heart
to see and love like you.
Help me to see in the way you see.
Help me to love like you love.
I pray for those whom I have thought of as "the enemy".
May they know their value.
May they know your love.
May they be blessed.

Prayer suggestion:

Make a list of all those whom you consider an enemy of some kind—whether you know them personally or you just know about them. Pray for them. Ask God for the eyes to see them and a heart to love them.

Prayer as Living in Love

God created us in love. God sustains us in love. God invites us into a relationship of love. The two great commandments are invitations to a life of love. These are the two pillars of wisdom that teach us who we are, who God is and who our neighbors are. These are the instructions that lie at the heart of the universe: "Love the Lord your God and love your neighbor as yourself." "Do this and you will live," Jesus said. Do this and you are living. This is life.

When we open our hearts in love to God who loves us, and open our hearts to all others, we are changed. The way we live is changed. We discover meaning, purpose and joy. We come alive.

We see others with new eyes. Our lives and words become a blessing, a humble gift, a kindness. Our spirits become open to receive words and deeds of blessing from others. We seek to practice fairness and mercy and to be builders of peace in our world. We find joy in serving others. We live more and more in God's love and God's love lives more and more in us.

In all these ways our lives become prayer. The giving and receiving of love is our prayer. Acts of kindness, of service, of blessing are our living prayer—the life and breath of God breathed out through us to others.

Seeing Others Through Eyes of Love

Then he {Jesus} turned toward the woman and said to
Simon, "Do you see this woman?"
Luke 7:44

The transformative power of prayer has the potential to change everything. As we place ourselves before God, God begins to give us new hearts. And God begins to give us new eyes. Our hearts become tender and vulnerable, like God's own heart of love. And our eyes begin to see others, no longer through the lenses of fear, competition or judgement, but through God's eyes of love.

This text is taken from a story in Luke's Gospel in which Jesus goes to dinner at Simon's home. Simon was a religious leader, a Pharisee. During the meal, a woman who "had lived a sinful life" came in and stood at Jesus' feet. She had heard that Jesus was at Simon's home and came specifically to see Jesus.

It seems likely that this woman had already had an encounter with Jesus during which she had experienced being seen and loved in a way she had never experienced before. This encounter with Jesus must have changed everything for her. She was probably accustomed to being viewed as an object to be used or judged. But, having encountered Jesus, she had been seen through eyes of love. Jesus had shown her who she really was. Not an object to be scorned. But a much loved child of God. Now she came in search of Jesus to express her profound gratitude.

This woman's tender gratitude was expressed in tears wept at Jesus' feet, in the kissing of his feet and with perfume poured out on his feet. She had been seen and loved, and as a result, her heart was broken open and overflowing with love for Jesus. But

Simon could not see this woman. He could not see her as the beloved child of God that she was. Instead, Simon saw her as a "sinner." An object of judgement. Someone who was "less-than".

Jesus addresses Simon's blindness directly. "Simon," Jesus says, "do you see this woman?" Do you see her love? Do you see her heart? I see her. I see her love. I see her through God's eyes of love. She is God's beloved daughter.

When we realize that God sees us through eyes of love we are profoundly healed. When we begin to see others through God's eyes of love, we bring healing and blessing to them. To be seen and loved, and to absorb the reality of that love, is to know ourselves for who we really are. And to know this is to be freed from self condemnation. To know this is to be made whole.

Imagine what it might be like to know that God sees us through eyes of love. Imagine what it might be to see others in this way. All others. People who are known to be "sinners". People who are self-righteous religious leaders. People who are well educated, people who are not. People who live in poverty. People who are wealthy. People of all nationalities and creeds. All loved by God. Each a treasure to God's heart.

I didn't see her.
I was blind.
I saw her only as a problem to be solved.
I didn't see the treasure.
I didn't see the love.
Your question was what I needed:
"Do you see this person?"
The answer was obvious.
She is precious, valued.
Loved.
And loving.
Grant me eyes to see the way you see.
Help me to see others through your eyes of love.

Prayer suggestion:

Ask God to bring someone to mind whom you need to see through God's eyes of love.

Ask God to help you see them with God's eyes of love.

Let your prayer be this new vision.

Ask God to expand your capacity to see all others in this way.

Blessing Others as Prayer

May the Lord answer you when you are in distress;
may the name of the God of Jacob protect you.
Psalm 20:1

Blessing others with our words and with our actions is a powerful form of prayer. When we express gratitude, we offer the prayer of blessing. When we affirm the gifts and the good we see in another person we offer the prayer of blessing. When we envision a hopeful future, we offer the prayer of blessing. When we treat others with respect and kindness, we offer the prayer of blessing.

Many of us have become accustomed to words and actions that discourage and destroy rather than words that build up and encourage. The shame associated with these words and actions can easily become internalized as a kind of self-condemnation or self-loathing. This leaves us with a private internal despair, seeing our contributions as insignificant, seeing ourselves as of little value, or seeing our futures as bleak.

Words and actions of blessing have the power, over time, to do the opposite. They have the power to heal, the power to strengthen, the power to bring hope.

Blessing is not the same as flattery, it is not the same as trying to change someone's mood by inflating their egos. Words and actions of blessing are always grounded in reality. The more we see other people as loved and valued by God and the more we trust that God actively cares for each human being, the more our eyes open to see others through eyes of love and respect.

The waiter that just brought us coffee is of infinite value. The person who is checking our groceries is deeply loved. Our friend is a delight to God.

Each person we encounter is a treasure. When we see this, we are more likely to listen attentively to others' needs. We are more likely to look for ways to offer genuine hope and affirmation to people in our lives. We are more likely to come along side others to provide compassionate care and support.

The prayer of blessing is sometimes offered spontaneously and sometimes it is offered more formally. A more formal prayer of blessing might be, for example, something we write in a birthday card, or a note at Thanksgiving. Or it might be something we express in a thoughtful act of kindness.

Words and actions are powerful. They can tear down. Or they can build up.

May we offer the prayer of blessing to others with words and actions that express gratitude, affirmation and hope today.

Give me eyes to see the way you see.
Help me to see the value in each of your children.
Help me to see through eyes of love and hope.
Help me to learn how to offer prayers of blessing
that flow naturally from my heart and mind.
And help me to listen to your words of blessing over me.
Precious, valuable, important, loved.
I know that as I take in these blessings,
I will grow in my capacity to pray blessings on others.

Prayer suggestion:

Ask God to bring someone to mind that you might bless in some way.

Ask God to show you if your words or actions have been hurtful rather than helpful to this person.

Ask God for the eyes to see this person through eyes of love and hope.

Ask God for words or actions of blessing that might be appropriate for this person.

When you can, share these words or deeds of blessing with this person.

Receiving from Others as Prayer

The Lord bless you and keep you;
the Lord make his face shine upon you
and be gracious to you;
the Lord turn his face toward you
and give you peace.
Numbers 6: 24-26

Prayer includes actively receiving words and deeds of blessing. Strangely enough this is something we sometimes resist. When people thank us for something we did or said that touched their lives in some way we may dismiss the blessing. Or someone might offer affirmations of our character, of our courage or perseverance. And again, we may reject this gift of blessing. Or someone might speak hopefully to us about our future, of things that God may do through us and for us. And we may push away this gift of hope regarding our personal future. Or someone might offer to help us in some way when we are in need, and we may feel hesitant to receive their kindness as a blessing.

Blessings are words and deeds that affirm our value as a person. Blessings are celebrations of who we are. Blessings can also be gifts of envisioning the future as a place where God meets us and gives us peace and grace.

We are meant to receive blessings from each other. It is important for us to learn to do this. But many of us are blocked from doing so because of the shame we have experienced. We may see ourselves as unworthy, as someone who doesn't measure up, as failures.

There are three practices that can help us receive blessings from others. First, we can look people in the eyes when they affirm us or thank us or extend a kindness to us. Secondly, we can begin to listen carefully to what people are saying when they speak words of blessing. And thirdly, we can respond by saying "Thank you," as if we were receiving a very thoughtful gift from this person. Because the truth is that when someone blesses us in word or deed they are giving us a significant gift.

If we see the act of receiving blessings as a form of prayer it might help us be more intentional about opening our hearts to these gifts. God blesses us directly in God's own words and actions of affirmation. But God also blesses us through the words and deeds of others. God sends us blessings through others to help us see ourselves through God's eyes of love and to help us to see the future as a place where God will be with us, helping us, guiding us and filling us with peace.

Teach me to receive words and deeds of blessing.
Teach me to see myself and my future through these blessings.
Replace my shame and self condemnation
with a growing awareness that
I am your beloved child.
Replace my fear and despair
with a vision of you providing for me.
Give me the grace and humility
to receive words and deeds of blessing
from others.
May my receiving from others in this way
be my prayer.

Prayer suggestion:

Sit quietly, take a few deep breaths and ask God to bring to your mind the smiles of people who care about you, the delight in people's eyes when they have greeted you, the words and deeds of affirmation that people have offered you. Ask God to give you the grace to receive these blessings.

Practice actively receiving words and deeds of affirmation and appreciation as gifts meant to heal and bless you.

Seeking Justice and Mercy as Prayer

He has showed you, O man, what is good.
And what does the Lord require of you?
To act justly and to love mercy
and to walk humbly with your God.
Micah 6:8

Prayer is more than our conversations with God. It is our life with God. Prayer is the life we live, the daily choices we make, the justice and mercy we show. These words from the prophet Micah are God's response to a series of questions Micah had thrown out at God. What does it mean to live in relationship with you, God? What is it that you ask of us? Micah then continued with what seems like an outburst of frustration with God, as if God were impossible to please. "Will the Lord be pleased with thousands of rams, with ten thousand rivers of oil?", Micah asked. Micah was asking if God wants us to be extreme in our worship and extreme in our sacrifice. What is required? What is enough? Is anything ever enough?

God's answer to this question is startlingly simple and clear. "What I am calling you to do is to walk humbly with me. Rely on me. Learn from me. Let me guide you in all of life. The outcome will be that I will teach you to love. I will teach you to love as I love. I will teach you act justly and to love mercy."

To act justly is to act in fairness. It means that we will repent of our greed and self centeredness. It means that we will care for the poor. It means that we will be a voice for those whose voices are not heard—the homeless, the refugee, the mentally ill, the marginalized, the young, the old, the widow, the orphan, the oppressed.

To love mercy is to be compassionate, forgiving, tender

hearted, kind. It is to repent of our judgmental ways, our lack of forgiveness, our hardheartedness. It means that we will see the value of each person even if they do not see our value—or their own.

Acting justly and loving mercy are descriptions of God. It is God who reveals to us over and over again in Scripture, and in Jesus, that God sees and cares for the poor, the homeless, the orphan, the widow. It is God who declares over and over again in Scripture, and in Jesus, that God is compassionate, forgiving and tender hearted toward all.

This text in Micah is echoed throughout Scripture. When we live in relationship with God, when we walk humbly with God, God transforms us. We become more and more like God. God creates in us the vision, the desire, the capability to live in love. We will grow in our care for those who are outcast or have no voice, because God's life is in us, moving through us. We will grow in our capacity to be compassionate, forgiving and tender hearted, because God's light is shining in us and through us.

This transformed and transforming life is a life of prayer. It is prayer in motion. It is prayer moving out into the world around us, in kindness, compassion and fairness toward all.

Prayer is not about religious performance, is it?
It's not about jumping through religious hoops.
Prayer is about walking hand-in-hand with you
like the child I am.
You ask me to give myself to you.
You ask me to live
in humility before you,
seeking your wisdom, your will, your way,
which is always the way of love.
Teach me to pray for justice
Teach me to do justice.
Teach me to pray for mercy.
Teach me to do mercy.
Teach me to pray for compassion and tender heartedness.
Teach me to live in compassion and tender heartedness.
Teach me to pray with my life
Make my life a prayer.

Prayer suggestion:

In a time of quiet see yourself, hand-in-hand with God, walking in the trust and humility of a much loved child. Ask for wisdom about the areas of your life in which God is specifically inviting you to act justly and to love tenderly today. Pray for the knowledge of God's will for you today and for the strength to carry it out.

Serving as Prayer

Jesus answered, "It is written:
'Worship the Lord your God
and serve him only.'"
Luke 4:8

When we pray, we open our hearts and minds to the God of love. Prayer allows us to experience God's active love directly. And prayer draws us into serving this One who is love. Our service, then, becomes a form of prayer.

Unfortunately, however, not all acts of service are acts of serving the God of love. Sometimes our acts of service are driven by fears that we need to placate an angry god. Sometimes our acts of service are driven by deep shame. Some are primarily attempts to make ourselves look good or feel good about ourselves. These acts of service are really attempts to serve our own interests.

Prayer is intended to be a kind of communion with and worship of God who is Love. Prayer opens us to the flow of God's love and grace. The experience of God's grace changes us and changes our acts of service. Instead of serving out of fear or shame, we are freed to serve from a place of gratitude, humility and joy. Knowing we are loved, we find ourselves able more and more to act out of love for others. Because we experience deeply the grace being given to us, we are empowered to extend grace to others.

Prayer is not, then, just about our times alone with God. In solitude we encounter our own need and God's grace in ways that prepare us and direct us to be a part of the flow of that grace to others. Henri Nouwen wrote, "In solitude we discover that our life is not a possession to be defended, but a gift to be shared." (Henri Nouwen, *Out of Solitude*. Ave Maria Press,

Notre Dame, 1974, p 22)

The prayer that empowers our service is a joyful, humbling, deeply moving kind of prayer. In this kind of prayer, God's grace fills us, pours out to others and comes back to bless us and fill us even more. The prayer of service is the prayer of love in action. In this sense, it could be said that Jesus' life, which was a life of service, was a continuous prayer.

"Follow me," Jesus calls to us. Let your life become a prayer. Give yourself to God so that God's life can flow in you and through you to bring healing and help to others. This sacred work of service to God and to others will give back to you and will profoundly enrich your life. For "when you serve the least of these," Jesus said, "you are serving me."

Help my life become a life of prayer.
Teach me to give myself to you,
that I might receive your Life and Love more fully every day,
Help me to serve you in ways that make it possible
for your Life and Love
to flow freely through me to others.
In serving you alone, God,
I find the freedom to give myself humbly and gracefully to others.
Show me how you would have me serve you today.

Prayer suggestion:

As you surrender yourself and your day to God, invite God to guide you in whatever acts of service God has for you today. Keep in mind these acts may be as simple as washing the dishes or calling a friend. Or they may be acts that require courage or special grace. Whatever acts you are guided to today, may they be acts of serving the One who loves you and loves us all. Know that your acts of service are a form of prayer.

Joining Hands and Voices as Prayer

They devoted themselves to the apostles teaching
and to fellowship, to the breaking of bread
and to prayer.
Acts 2: 42

Sometimes prayer is joining hands and voices in worship, in petition, in confession, in grief and in joy. Praying with others reminds us that when we pray, whether we are by ourselves or in a congregation of worshippers, we never really pray alone. Prayer always joins our spirits with God's Spirit and with the spirits of others. Prayer is always an act of communion with a larger community.

When we physically join hands and voices with others in prayer we experience in a direct way that we are a part of a family, that we are interconnected and interdependent. The effects of this experience in prayer are many. First, our faith is often strengthened by the faith of those with whom we pray. We draw on each other's experience, strength and hope. Second, we feel less isolated. We have the opportunity to directly experience our spiritual connection with other people. Thirdly, the Spirit sometimes chooses to move, teach, heal and counsel in ways that may not happen when we are by ourselves in prayer. When we join hands and voices with tender hearts and teachable spirits we invite the Spirit to be present with us in powerful ways.

It is important to keep in mind some of the potential pitfalls of praying with others. There is a temptation when we are praying with others to try to impress. We may want to sound spiritual or pious. We may want to use the occasion to preach rather than to pray. We may find ourselves unwilling to pray with the vulnerability and lack of pretense that prayer requires. These pitfalls do not need to rob us of the experience of praying with others. When we find ourselves slipping into one of these dysfunctional modes of prayer we can experience it as a reminder to ask for a spirit of humility as we pray with others.

Many of the ways of relating to God that solitary prayer offers are experiences that can be shared with others as we come together to pray. The experience of praying with others can include the prayer of praise, of confession, of contemplative silence, of joyful song, of reading together from a book of prayer or from Scripture, of intercession, or of spontaneous conversation with God.

Faith communities may be made up of two or three individuals, or of many hundreds or even thousands of individuals. Whatever the numbers might be, we are most receptive to the presence of God's healing love and grace when we join hands and voices in acknowledgment of our brokenness and our need, and when we come together seeking the forgiveness, help and strength we need to live the lives of love we are called by God to live.

We join our hands and voices,
acknowledging our need of you,
seeking your grace,
asking to know your Presence with us.
Forgive us.
Heal us.
Teach us.
Fill us.
Make us yours.
Together we give ourselves to you.
Together we raise our voices in joyful song.
We praise you because you are Love
and your love endures forever.

Prayer suggestion:

Reflect prayerfully for a few moments on your experiences of praying with others.

What blessings do you see? What pitfalls are you aware of?

Ask God to enrich your times of prayer with others.

Seek some opportunity to join hands and voices with others in prayer.

Prayer as Joy and Celebration

Sometimes prayer is having a party. Prayer can be putting on the music and dancing and shouting for joy. Prayer is receiving honor and glory from God. Prayer is breaking into smiles and saying "Thank you!" to God. Prayer is singing songs of joyful love to our Maker.

For those of us who think of prayer as a burden, or who picture prayer as something that happens in cold, dank churches in moments of desperation, this idea of prayer could be startling. It is like throwing open all the shutters and allowing the light of a beautiful day to stream into our darkened souls.

Prayer is the expression of joy because there is reason for joy. We are loved. We are called to love. Life has meaning. We are a part of Someone greater than ourselves. We are a part of each other. We are blessed. We are called to be a part of that blessing to others.

"Have a party!" God says to us. "Celebrate!" "Enjoy!" "Dance, shout, sing, make music, have a good time. Pray."

God, the breath of Life, breathes into us and we live. God pursues us in love. God heals us, forgives us, corrects us, guides us, sings for joy over us. And invites us to celebrate the deepest joy of all: we are loved. We are valued. Life is a gift to be received, shared, celebrated.

Prayer is lived out in joy. Prayer is celebration.

Practicing Gratitude as Prayer

Give thanks to the Lord for he is good;
his love endures forever.
Psalm 118:1

Give thanks! God is good! God's love endures forever! The Lord is good. The Lord's love is constant, strong, enduring. We give thanks in acknowledgment of this goodness and this unshakable love. We give thanks to celebrate these most fundamental truths about our Maker.

Some of us hesitate to express gratitude to God. Our capacity to express gratitude may have been compromised by relationships in which the expression of gratitude was an obligation, or it may have functioned as a way of communicating that we were unworthy in some way. Gratitude is never an obligation, it is a response to Love. Gratitude does not come from a sense of worthlessness, but from a growing sense that we are greatly valued by God.

What the psalmist emphasizes in this text is that God's love for us is abundant, unfailing, beyond comprehension. It is out of tender, powerful love for us that God gives us good gifts.

This is how Jesus put it: "Which of you fathers, if your son asks for a fish, will give him a snake instead? Or if he asks for an egg, will give him a scorpion? If you then, though you are evil, know how to give good gifts to your children, how much more will your Father in heaven give the Holy Spirit to those who ask him!" (Luke 11:11-13).

Like a loving parent, God sees us through eyes of delight and joy. God sees us through eyes of love and valuing. It is with joy that God gives to us. It is out of an endless abundance of love for us that God blesses us. It is because of who God is that we give thanks.

God is good and always, always loving. It is Love that makes it possible for us to open our hearts in gratitude and express our thankfulness to God for all we have been given.

As we do this on a regular basis, something begins to happen to us. We begin to notice more and more of the gifts we are being given. We begin to trust more fully the Giver of those good gifts. The reality of God's goodness and love begin to take root in our hearts. As a result, our ability to rest in God's love and goodness deepens.

Give thanks to God, for God is good.

Give thanks to God, for God's love endures forever.

For your goodness, I give thanks.
For your enduring love, I give thanks.
For your attentiveness, I give thanks.
For your purposes of joy, I give thanks.
For who you are, I give thanks.
For who you are to me, I give thanks.
I open my heart in gratitude and joy.

Prayer suggestion:

Ask God to open your heart in gratitude for who God is.

Ask God to open your heart in gratitude for all you have received.

Spend some time expressing your gratitude to God.

Write your own psalm of gratitude for who God is.

Finish by writing a gratitude list of some of the many gifts you have been given.

Make a practice of writing gratitude lists on a regular basis.

Experiencing Glory as Prayer

O Lord, how many are my foes!
How many rise up against me!
Many are saying of me,
"God will not deliver him."
But you are a shield around me, O Lord,
you bestow glory on me and lift up my head.
Psalm 3:1-3

We all know what it is like to feel judged by others. And what it is like when we judge ourselves. We know how painful it is to feel like we are defective. We know what it is like to be treated—by others and by ourselves—as if we have little or no value. We know what it is like to have people tell us that we have no value in God's eyes, that "God will not deliver" us.

These experiences are an astonishing contrast to the perspective offered in this psalm. Others may treat us as if we have little value, and we may treat ourselves as if we have little value. But God is a shield around us, God bestows glory on us and lifts up our head.

We may bow our heads in shame, but God lifts up our heads. We may experience voices around us and within us that accuse us or devalue us, but God bestows glory.

Glory is a word that is used in Scripture primarily about God. God's glory is God's beauty and splendor. God's glory is God's goodness, power and love. So to read this word in relation to ourselves is stunning.

In a later psalm we read that God values humankind so much that God "crowns him with glory and honor" (Psalm 8:5). In the New Testament we read that we are being "transformed into his likeness with ever increasing glory." (2 Corinthians 3:18)

God has not forgotten the beauty, the goodness, the glory which God placed within us. We are created in God's own image—a great and lasting dignity that nothing can take away. This honor and glory is not something we earn. It is not a prize we can win. It is the gift we have been given by God.

God has not forgotten the glory that has been given to each of us. God shields and protects our worth. God crowns us with glory and honor.

Prayer opens us to the One who is a shield around us, protecting the beauty and worth that God has placed in each of us. Prayer opens us to the One who lifts up our head and bestows honor and glory on us. Prayer is receiving and knowing the glory given to us by God.

There are many voices around me and within me.
Some judge me. Some find me inadequate.
Some tell me that I have no value.
Some tell me that you do not care.
But you, God, shield me.
You know better than anyone how I fail and fall.
You know better than anyone my weakness and pride.
But you have not forgotten the glory,
the light, the beauty that you placed in me
when you made me.
When my head is bowed in shame,
you lift up my head.
You restore my dignity. You affirm my worth.
You bestow honor on me, You crown me with glory.
Help me to experience the glory today.
Help me to be who you made me to be.

Prayer suggestion:

Spend some time identifying the judgments you experience
from others and from yourself. Notice how these weigh you
down and rob you of your sense of dignity and worth. Ask God
to help you see and experience the shield of loving protection
God places around you. Ask God to allow you to experience
having your head lifted up as God crowns you with glory.

Being Open to Joy as Prayer

As the Father has loved me, so have I loved you.
Now remain in my love. If you obey my commandments,
you will remain in my love, just as I have obeyed my
Father's commands and remain in his love.
I have told you this so that my joy may be in you
and that your joy may be complete.
My commandment is this,
love each other
as I have loved you.
John 15: 9-12

Jesus told his followers that he wanted them to experience his joy. And that the experience of joy comes from living in the flow of God's love. Jesus began this teaching saying something like this: "I love you. In the same tender, unshakeable way that God the Father loves me, I love you. This reality is the foundation for all of life. This reality is the source of joy. You are loved. Rest in this love. Stay close to me and to my love for you."

Joy comes as we open ourselves to God's love for us and as we rest in that reality.

For some of us, the process of opening to God's love is a long, long journey. For most of us, it is a process full of challenges. We may believe in a God of love, but privately fear that God is distant, disapproving or harsh. Or we may fear that somehow we are unlovable, unreachable or not included.

God actively seeks to heal our fears so that we can be free to rest in God's unfailing love. Our part is to ask, and to keep asking, for eyes to see and a heart to receive the gift of God's love for us. Our part is to ask for the grace to "remain in this love," to stay close to this love, to let our roots sink deeply into the soil of this love.

Jesus continued his teaching about joy by calling us to love others. It is helpful to notice the order of this teaching. First, we are told that we are loved. Then we are told to remain in the reality of that love. And then we are called to love each other.

As we begin to take in God's love and to rest in God's love, we begin to change. We are better able to let God's love fill us and guide us. As a result, we begin to see others as God sees them, through eyes of love. In this way, God's love begins to flow through us to others. We change how we view others and how we act toward others.

This short teaching captures much of the essence of life. We are deeply, abundantly loved by God. As we rest in that love we are filled with the joy of Christ and we are freed to love as we have been loved.

We all seek happiness, meaning and security in life. Jesus shows us the key to all of this and to the gift of abundant joy. "Know that I love you. Remain in my love for you. Sink your roots deeply into my love for you. Let my love change you. Let my love flow through you to others. In this way you will be able to love others as I love you. And my joy will live in you, making your joy complete." Staying open to joy, by remaining in love, is prayer.

You love me.
Give me the grace to rest in that love,
Help me to sink my roots deeply into the soil of your love.
Give me the grace to live a life of surrender to your love,
Fill me with love so that love flows through me to others.
Help me to know the joy
of remaining in your love
and of being a channel for your love.
Let your joy fill me.

Prayer suggestion:

Reflect on times of joy when you have experienced both the grace of knowing God's love for you and of allowing that love to guide how you treat others. Ask God to increase your ability to "remain in God's love." Ask God to free you to be open to the joy that comes as you rest in God's love and as you allow that love to flow through you to others.

Singing Love Songs to God as Prayer

I love the Lord, for he heard my voice;
he heard my cry for mercy.
Because he turned his ear to me,
I will call on him as long as I live.
The Lord is gracious and righteous,
our God is full of compassion.
Psalm 116:1,2,9

Sometimes prayer is a love song to God. It may be a song we sing, or words of gratitude we speak, or deep unspoken joy. As our eyes open to God's faithful love, as our hearts take in the reality of God's love more and more, we may find our spirits singing love songs to our Maker. These love songs can be our prayer.

Many of the psalms read like personal love songs to God. Many of them tell a story of a time when the psalmist experienced a great grief or desperate need. Often the suffering is described in some detail. And then, the story shifts. God acts. God rescues, heals, helps, saves. And the psalmist's terrible distress is eased. Despair gives way to hope. Sorrow gives way to joy. And the psalmist sings songs of love to God.

Reading the psalms can teach us the language of the heart, the language of emotions, the language of love. Reading the psalms can give us words to express our own love songs to God.

Many of us have stories that are much like the stories told in the psalms. Many of us have experienced times of great grief or desperate need and have cried out to God for help. Many of us have experienced God acting in love to meet our personal need. Perhaps we didn't even cry out to God. Perhaps we were unable to speak. But God acted. God's light shown in our darkness,

God's kindness rescued us and gave us hope.

These moments of grace are moments of tender encounter with the living God. They change us. They alter the course of our lives. And our hearts have a need to sing about the love and gratitude we experience.

Let your heart sing its love songs to God. Sing your story of God's personal love for you. Sing your gladness. Sing your gratitude. Sing your love and joy to God.

I was in desperate need,

sinking in a dark pit.

I cried out to you and waited for you.

And you acted.

You took my hand

and pulled me out of the pit.

You set me on a solid rock.

You rescued me.

You did for me what I could not do for myself.

And in it all I experienced more fully

your love for me.

I love you.

My heart sings with love for you.

I love you, God.

I love you.

Prayer suggestion:

Read a favorite psalm. Or begin reading through the psalms, learning this language of the heart.

As you are ready, write, or sing, or speak your own love song to God.

Celebrating as Prayer

Then all the people went away to eat and drink,
to send portions of food
and to celebrate with great joy,
because they now understood the words
that had been made known to them.
Nehemiah 8:12

The context of this text is that the people of Israel had been released from captivity. They have just listened together to words from Scripture. They have listened to words inviting them into a relationship with God, inviting them to be God's people and to let God be their God.

Because of the long years of captivity, they had not heard these words of good news for many years. They may have questioned or forgotten that they were loved by God. But now they heard these life giving words again. And they understood.

The people were so moved by what they heard that they wept. They may have been weeping in joy. Or weeping over the years during which they had been deprived of their freedom and of the good news of God's love for them. Or weeping because it all seemed too good to be true.

But whatever their reasons were for weeping, their leaders wanted them to take in the good news of God's love by celebrating. So their leaders told them: "Enjoy choice food and sweet drinks and send some to those who have nothing prepared...For the joy of the Lord is our strength." (Nehemiah 8:10).

And, so the people responded to this direction and celebrated with joy. Sometimes prayer is like that—like celebration. Sometimes prayer is literally having a party.

We may not look like we are praying when we are celebrating, but it can be an act of prayer. It can be an act of receiving and acknowledging the gifts that God gives us. The eating of "choice foods" and the "drinking of sweet drinks" and the sharing of food and drink with others in grateful celebration can be a way of saying "Yes!" and "Thank you!" to God.

When we celebrate with choice foods at Thanksgiving or Christmas or Easter, or at any other time, it is not only the moments when we say grace that is our prayer. The sharing of the "choice foods and sweet drinks" is also our prayer.

This is also true on special occasions like holidays and birthdays. And it can be true on ordinary days as well. When we slice a piece of bread and make a cup of tea and share these things with others we are celebrating our life in God. When we are aware of these gifts, when we are mindful that every day is an opportunity to take in God's blessing, we enter the prayer of celebration.

Celebration is an active expression of our joy in response to God who is love. This particular prayer strengthens us. For "the joy of the Lord is our strength."

A party?
Really?
You want me to take in
your goodness and love
by having a party?
"Go make some choice food," you say.
And "have some people over."
"Celebrate," you say.
You invite me to express the joy
that comes from knowing you
by enjoying good food with others.
I can do this.
I can pray like this.
I will celebrate.
Help me to let the joy I find in knowing you
be my strength today.

Prayer suggestion:

Plan a party. Prepare you favorite foods and invite some people over. Or simply prepare some tea or coffee and a snack to share. Let this celebration be your prayer of joy. Let this joy give you new strength.

Dancing and Shouting for Joy as Prayer

Praise the LORD.
Praise God in his sanctuary;
praise him in his mighty heavens.
praise him with tambourine and dancing,
praise him with the strings and flute,
Let everything that has breath praise the LORD.
Praise the LORD. Psalm 150:1,4,6

Sometimes we suffer not only from denying and suppressing grief, but also from denying and suppressing joy. Joy, like grief, is a physical experience. It is an emotion that carries a great deal of energy—energy that begs to be released. In grief, this release is usually found in tears. In joy this release is often found in making music, shouting and dancing.

Sometimes prayer is about shouting for joy and dancing.

Something wonderful happens when we play music and raise our arms and move our feet and shout our joy about the gifts we have been given. As we dance we can shout out our words of gratitude. "Thank you, God, for life today! Thank you, God, that you are with us! Thank you, God, for your love!"

This kind of activity allows us to take in the gifts that are continually given to us. This kind of prayer grounds us in our body and in the breathtaking gift of the moment. We need to do more of this. For life is precious and the gifts we are given often go under appreciated, under celebrated, under enjoyed.

People who are faced with life threatening illnesses sometimes experience moments when their eyes seem to be opened to see that heaven is here on earth. Colors may suddenly be brighter. Life itself may feel heart breaking in its sweetness. The act of breathing is understood to be a miracle. There may be a sense of being given glimpses of the beauty and wonder of all that normally seems ordinary. And in these moments it seems clear that it would be appropriate to shout for joy with each breath.

Shouting and dancing in joyful praise for all we have been given and all we are being given brings our minds, our bodies and our spirits into a place of grateful wholeness. It heals our despair, our lethargy, our dullness. It awakens us more deeply to the reality of God's goodness and care for us.

Many of us were raised to constrict our movements and our noise making. Many of us were raised in cultures which had strong constraints on the expression of emotion. But such constraints do not apply in God's family. It is time to turn up the music and to put on some dancing shoes. Shouting and dancing for joy is blessed. It is a form of prayer to which God invites us.

I shout to you who can hear my faintest whisper.
I sing to you who sings so tenderly over me.
I dance for joy, God of the dance.
For all you have done.
For all you are doing.
For all your good gifts and loving care.
I shout my praise to you.
I dance in joy for you.

Prayer suggestion:

Put on some of your favorite music and shout your joy while you dance in praise for God's good gifts—and for God whose love endures forever.

Other Books of Meditations by Juanita Ryan

Life is full of challenges—sometimes overwhelming ones. Juanita Ryan is no stranger to times like this. In *Keep Breathing: What to Do When You Can't Figure Out What to Do* Juanita writes from personal experience about the things that helped her to navigate the complexities of some of the most challenging seasons in life.

If you are recovering from addiction, abuse or trauma, then *Rooted in God's Love: Meditations on Biblical Texts for People in Recovery* will be a source of encouragement, support and strength.

Both of these books are available from online retailers.

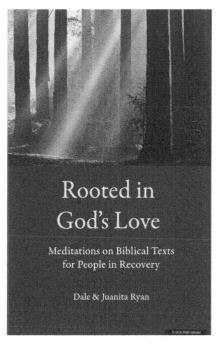

Made in the USA
Monee, IL
27 February 2023

28820251R10193